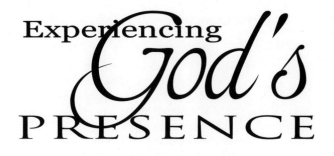

Experiencing God's PRESENCE

Matthew Henry

**WHITAKER
HOUSE**

Publisher's note:
This new edition from Whitaker House has been updated for the
modern reader. Words, expressions, and sentence structure have
been revised for clarity and readability.

All Scripture quotations are from the King James Version (KJV) of
the Holy Bible.

EXPERIENCING GOD'S PRESENCE

ISBN: 0-88368-844-1
Printed in the United States of America
© 1997 by Whitaker House

Whitaker House
30 Hunt Valley Circle
New Kensington, PA 15068
www.whitakerhouse.com

Library of Congress Cataloging-in-Publication Data

Henry, Matthew, 1662–1714.
Experiencing God's presence / Matthew Henry.
p.   cm.
Originally published: New Kensington, PA : Whitaker
House, © 1997.
ISBN 0-88368-844-1 (pbk.)
1. Spiritual life—Christianity.   I. Title.
BV4501.3 .H46 2002
248.4—dc21
2002012142

2 3 4 5 6 7 8 9 10 11 **ⱳ** 10 09 08 07 06 05 04

Contents

Chapter 1

Beginning Every Day with God

*My voice shalt thou hear in the
morning, O Lord.*
—Psalm 5:3

I wish to recommend to you David's example
in this text. He had resolved in Psalm 5:2 that
he would abound in and abide by the duty
of prayer: *"Unto thee will I pray."* Then, in verse
three, he set one proper time for it, and that is
the morning: *"My voice shalt thou hear in the
morning."* However, it was not only in the morning that David prayed, for he solemnly undertook
the duty of prayer three times a day, as Daniel did:
*"Evening, and morning, and at noon, will I pray,
and cry aloud"* (Ps. 55:17). No, he did not even
think that was enough, for he said, *"Seven times*

a day do I praise thee" (Ps. 119:164). But I wish to focus particularly on the morning.

I will show that it is our wisdom and duty to begin every day with God. Let us observe in the words of our text, first, the good work itself that we are to do. God must hear our voices; we must direct our prayers to Him. Let us observe, second, the special time appointed and observed for the doing of this good work—in the morning, and again in the morning, that is, every morning, as consistently as morning comes.

The good work that David's example teaches us to do is, in one word, to pray. It is a duty dictated by the light and law of nature, which plainly and loudly says, "Should a people not seek their God?" However, the Gospel of Christ gives us much better instructions and encouragements concerning prayer than any that nature furnishes us, for it tells us what we must pray for, in whose name we must pray, and by whose assistance. It invites us to *"come boldly unto the throne of grace"* (Heb. 4:16) and to *"enter into the holiest by the blood of Jesus"* (Heb. 10:19).

This work we are to do, not in the morning only, but at other times, at all times. We read of preaching the Word *"out of season"* (2 Tim. 4:2), but we do not read of praying out of season, for that is never out of season. The throne of grace is always open, and humble suppliants are always welcome and cannot come unseasonably.

"My Voice Shalt Thou Hear"

But let us see how David here expressed his pious resolutions to abide by this duty. David said, *"My voice shalt thou hear."* David may here be understood two different ways: either, *God will* hear my voice, or, *I will* faithfully pray to my God. Let us examine the first meaning; then we will examine the second.

God Will Hear

David promised himself a gracious acceptance with God: "You shall, that is, You *will* hear my voice when I direct my prayer to You in the morning." This is the language of his faith, grounded on God's promise, that His ear will always be open to the cry of His people. He had prayed, *"Give ear to my words, O Lord"* (Ps. 5:1), and, in the next verse, *"Hearken unto the voice of my cry."* And then, in verse three, he received an answer to those prayers, and he said, "You will hear, I do not doubt that You will; and though I do not have right now a grant of the thing I prayed for, yet I am sure my prayer is heard, is accepted, and comes up for a memorial, as the prayer of Cornelius did." (See Acts 10:4.) It is put in God's file and will not be forgotten. If we look inward and can say by experience that God has prepared our hearts, we may look upward, may look forward, and say with confidence that He will cause His ear to hear.

We may be sure of this, and we must pray in the assurance of it, that wherever God finds a praying heart, He will be found to be a prayer-hearing God. Even if the voice of prayer is a low voice, a weak voice, yet, if it comes from an upright heart, it is a voice that God will hear, that He will hear with pleasure. It is His delight, and He will return a gracious answer. He has heard your prayers; He has seen your tears.

Therefore, when we stand praying, we must stand on this principle, without doubting or wavering: Whatever we ask of God as a Father, in the name of Jesus Christ the Mediator, according to the will of God revealed in Scripture, it will be granted us either in kind or kindness. This is what is promised to us in John 16:23, and the truth of this promise is sealed to us by the concurring experience of the saints in all ages, ever since man began to call on the name of the Lord. Jacob's God never yet said to Jacob's seed, "You seek Me in vain," and He will not begin now. When we come to God by prayer, if we come rightly, we may be confident of this: that notwithstanding the distance between heaven and earth and our great unworthiness to have any favor shown us, yet God does hear our voices, and He will not turn away our prayers or His mercy.

I Will Faithfully Pray

Although Psalm 5:3 may be taken as a promise that God will hear our prayers, it is also to be taken as David's promising God a constant attendance upon Him in the way He has appointed. *"My voice shalt thou hear"*; that is, I will speak to You. Because You have inclined Your ear to me many a time, therefore I have taken up a resolution to call on You at all times, even to the end of my time. Not a day will pass without Your hearing from me.

Not that the voice is the thing that God regards, as those spoken of in Isaiah 58:4 seemed to think, who in prayer made their voice to be heard on high. Hannah prayed and prevailed when her voice was not heard. It is the voice of the heart that is meant here. God said to Moses, *"Wherefore criest thou unto me?"* (Exod. 14:15) when we do not read that he had said one word. Praying is lifting up the soul to God and pouring out the heart before Him.

As far as expressing the devout affections of the heart by words, they may be of use to focus our thoughts and to excite our desires. It is good to draw near to God, not only with a pure heart, but with a humble voice; in this way we must render *"the calves* [or the offerings] *of our lips"* (Hos. 14:2).

However, God understands the language of the heart, and that is the language in which we must speak to Him. David prayed not only, *"Give ear to my words,"* but, *"Consider my meditation"* (Ps. 5:1). Let the words of my mouth, proceeding from the meditation of my heart, be acceptable in Your sight (Ps. 19:14).

We must pray from our hearts in every prayer. We must speak to God; we must write to Him. If we receive a letter from a friend, we say that we have heard from him; we must see to it that God hears from us daily.

God Expects Our Prayers

God expects and requires our prayers. Though He does not need us or our services and cannot be benefited by them, He has obliged us to offer the sacrifice of prayer and praise to Him continually.

God requires us to pray for good reason. Thus God will keep us by His authority over us. He will keep us continually mindful of our subjection to Him, which we are apt to forget. He requires that by prayer we solemnly pay our homage to Him and give honor to His name. By this act and deed of homage, frequently repeated, we will strengthen our obligations to observe His statutes, keep His laws, and be more and more sensible of the weight of them. He is your Lord; worship Him. By frequent, humble adorations of His perfections, you will make a constant, humble compliance with

His will easier for yourself. By doing obeisance, we are learning obedience.

God's requirement that we pray is a testimony of His love and compassion toward us. If He had only said, "Let Me hear from you as often as there is occasion; call on Me in the time of trouble or need, and that is enough," He would have abundantly shown His concern and goodness. However, to show His pleasure in us, as a father does his affection to his child when he is sending him abroad, He gives us this charge: "Let me hear from you every day, though you have no particular business." He shows that *"the prayer of the upright is his delight"* (Prov. 15:8); it is music to His ears.

Christ says to His dove, *"Let me see thy countenance, let me hear thy voice; for sweet is thy voice, and thy countenance is comely"* (Song 2:14). And it is to the spouse, the church, that Christ speaks in the close of that song of songs: *"Thou that dwellest in the gardens, the companions hearken to thy voice: cause me to hear it"* (Song 8:13). What a shame it is to us that God is more willing to be prayed to and more ready to hear prayer than we are to pray!

We Have Something to Say

We have something to say to God every day. Many people are not aware of this, and it is their sin and misery; they live without God in the world. They think they can live without Him; they are not aware of their dependence on Him and their obligations to Him. Therefore, for their part, they have nothing to say to Him. He never hears from them, no more than the father did from his prodigal son when the son was away from home. They ask scornfully, "What can the Almighty do for me?" Then it is no marvel if they ask next, *"What profit should we have, if we pray unto him?"* (Job 21:15). And the result is that they say to the Almighty, *"Depart from us"* (Job 21:14), and this will be their doom.

But I hope better things of you, my fellow believers. I believe that you are not of those who restrain prayer before God. You are ready to acknowledge that there is a great deal that the Almighty can do for you, and that there is profit in praying to Him; therefore, you resolve to draw near to God that He may draw near to you (James 4:8).

We have something to say to God daily, as to a friend we love and have freedom with. We cannot pass the home of such a friend without calling on him; we never lack something to say to him, though we have no particular business with him. To such a friend we open up; we profess our love and esteem, and with pleasure communicate our thoughts. Abraham was called *"the Friend of God"* (James 2:23), and this honor belongs to all the saints. *"I call you not servants,"* says Christ, *"but I have called you friends"* (John 15:15). *"His secret is with the righteous"* (Prov. 3:32). We are invited to acquaint ourselves with Him and to walk with Him, as one friend walks with another. The fellowship of believers is said to be with the Father and with His Son Jesus Christ; and do we have nothing to say to Him then?

Is it not enough of an errand to go to the throne of His grace to admire His infinite perfections, which we can never fully comprehend, or sufficiently contemplate, or take enough pleasure in? Is it not enough of an errand to please ourselves in beholding the beauty of the Lord and to give Him the glory due to His name? Have we not a great deal to say to Him in acknowledgment of His condescending grace and favor to us in manifesting Himself to us and not to the world, and in profession of our affection and submission to Him? *"Lord, thou knowest all things; thou knowest that I love thee"* (John 21:17).

God has something to say to us as a friend every day, through His providences, through our own consciences, and through the written Word in which we must hear His voice. He hearkens and hears whether we have anything to say to Him by way of reply, and we are very unfriendly if we do not. When He says to us, *"Seek ye my face,"* should our hearts not answer as to one we love, *"Thy face, LORD, will I seek"* (Ps. 27:8)? When He says to us, *"Return, ye backsliding children,"* should we not readily reply, *"Behold, we come unto thee; for thou art the* L<small>ORD</small> *our God"* (Jer. 3:22)? If He speaks to us by way of conviction and reproof, should we not answer with confession and submission? If He speaks to us by way of comfort, should we not reply in praise? If you love God, you should not have to seek for something to say to Him, something for your heart to pour out before Him, which His grace has already put there.

We have something to say to God daily, not only as a friend, but also as a master whom we serve and with whom we have business. Think how numerous and important the concerns are that lie between us and God, and you will readily acknowledge that you have a great deal to say to Him. We have a constant dependence on Him. All our expectations are from Him. We have constant dealings with Him; He is the God *"with whom we have to do"* (Heb. 4:13).

Do we not know that our happiness is bound up in His favor, that His favor is life, the life of our souls? It is better than life, than the life of our bodies. And do we not have business with God to seek His favor, to entreat it with our whole hearts, to beg as for our lives that He would lift up the light of His countenance upon us? Do we not have business with God to plead Christ's righteousness, as that through which alone we can hope to obtain God's loving-kindness?

Do we not know that we have offended God, that by sin we have made ourselves liable to His wrath and curse and that we are daily contracting guilt? And then, do we not have business enough with Him to confess our faults and follies, to ask for pardon in the blood of Christ, to make our peace with God in Him who is our peace, and to renew our covenant with Him in His own strength to go and sin no more?

Do we not know that we have daily work to do for God and our own souls, the work of the day that is to be done in its day? We have business with God to beg of Him to show us what He wants us to do, to direct us in it, and to strengthen us for it. Should we not seek Him for assistance and acceptance that He would work in us both to will and to do that which is good (Phil. 2:13), and then accept and own His own work? Such business as this the servant has with his master.

Do we not know that we are continually in danger? Both the life and the comfort of our bodies are in danger. We are continually surrounded with disease and death, whose arrows fly at midnight and at midday. Do we not then have business with God, in our going out and coming in, in our lying down and rising up, to put ourselves under the protection of His providence, to be the charge of His holy angels?

Both the life and the comfort of our souls are in even more danger. It is our souls that our adversary the devil, a strong and subtle adversary, wars against and seeks to devour. Do we not then have business with God to put ourselves under the protection of His grace and gird ourselves with His armor so that we may be able to stand against the wiles and violences of Satan (Eph. 6:11)? Should we not arm ourselves so that we may neither be surprised into sin by a sudden temptation nor overpowered by a strong one?

Do we not know that we are dying daily, that death is working in us and hastening toward us, that death fetches us to judgment, and that judgment fixes us in our everlasting state? And do we not then have something to say to God in preparation of what is before us? We should say, *"'Lord, make me to know mine end'* (Ps. 39:4)! Lord, *'teach us to number our days'* (Ps. 90:12)!" Do we not have business with God to judge ourselves that we may not be judged (1 Cor. 11:31) and to see to it that our matters are right and good?

Do we not know that we are members of that body of which Christ is the head; and are we not concerned to prove ourselves living members? Do we not then have business with God upon the public account to make intercession for His church? Do we have nothing to say for Zion, nothing in behalf of Jerusalem's ruined walls, nothing for the peace and welfare of the land of our birth?

Are we not of the family, or but babes in it, that we do not concern ourselves in the concerns of it?

Do we have no relatives, no friends who are dear to us, whose joys and griefs we share? And do we have nothing to say to God for them, no complaints to make, no requests to make known? Are none of them sick or in distress, none of them tempted or downhearted? And do we not have errands at the throne of grace to beg relief and help for them?

Now put all this together, and then consider whether or not you have something to say to God every day. Particularly in days of trouble it is fitting to cry out to God. On these days you can say to God, *"I have borne chastisement"* (Job 34:31), and, if you have any sense of things, you will say, *"Do not condemn me"* (Job 10:2).

Allow No Hindrances

If you have all this to say to God, what should hinder you from saying it, from saying it every day? Why should He not hear your voice, when you have so many messages for Him?

Do not let distance hinder you from speaking with God. Imagine that you have occasion to speak with a friend, but he is a great way away. You cannot reach him; you do not know where to find him or how to get a letter to him. Therefore, your business with him is left undone.

But distance does not need to keep you from speaking to God; for though it is true that God is in heaven and we are on earth, yet He is near to His praying people in all that they call on Him for. He hears their voices wherever they are. *"Out of the depths have I cried unto thee"* (Ps. 130:1), said David. *"From the end of the earth will I cry unto thee"* (Ps. 61:2). Jonah said, *"Out of the belly of hell cried I, and thou heardest my voice"* (Jonah 2:2). In all places, we can find a way open heavenward. Thanks be to Him who by His own blood has consecrated for us a new and living way into the holiest and has established a correspondence between heaven and earth.

Do not let fear hinder you from saying what you have to say to God. Imagine that you have business with a great man, but he is so far above you, or so stern and severe toward all his inferiors, that you are afraid to speak to him. You have no one to introduce you or to speak a good word for you, and therefore you choose rather to drop your cause.

But there is no occasion for your being thus discouraged in speaking to God. You may come boldly to the throne of His grace; there you have a liberty of speech, permission to pour out your whole soul. And such are His compassions to humble suppliants, that even His terror does not need to make them afraid. God does not want you to frighten yourself! He would have you encourage yourself, *"for ye have not received the spirit of bondage again to fear; but ye have received the Spirit of adoption"* (Rom. 8:15). By adoption you are brought into, among other things, the glorious liberties of the children of God.

This is not all. We have someone to introduce us and to speak for us, an Advocate with the Father. Did children ever need an advocate with their father? But God has given us two immutable things, in which it is impossible for Him to lie, that *"we might have a strong consolation"* (Heb. 6:18): We have not only the relation of the Father to depend on, but also the interest and intercession of an Advocate, a High Priest over the house of God, in whose name we have access with confidence.

Do not let His knowing what your business is and what you have to say to Him hinder you. Imagine that you have business with a certain friend, but you do not think you need to trouble yourself about it for he is already informed of it. He knows what you want, but does that mean you do not need to speak with him?

It is true that all your desire is before God. He knows your needs and burdens. But He wants to hear them from you. He has promised you relief, but His promise must be put into a petition, and He will *"for this be inquired of by the house of Israel, to do it for them"* (Ezek. 36:37). Though we cannot through our prayers give Him any information, we must through our prayers give Him honor. It is true, nothing we say can have any influence on Him or move Him to show us mercy; but it may have an influence on ourselves and help put us into a position to receive mercy.

The following is a very easy and reasonable condition of His favors: *"Ask, and it shall be given you"* (Matt. 7:7). It was to teach us the necessity of praying in order to receive favor that Christ put that strange question to the blind man: *"What wilt thou that I should do unto thee?"* (Mark 10:51). He knew what he wanted, but those who touch the top of the golden scepter must be ready to state their petition and their request.

We must not let any other business hinder our saying what we have to say to God. We may have business with a friend that we cannot accomplish because we do not have the time. Perhaps we have something else to do that we think is more important. But we cannot say so concerning the business we have with God, for that is without a doubt the one necessary thing to which everything else must be made to give way.

It is not at all necessary to our happiness that we be great in the world or that we amass a large estate; but it is absolutely necessary that we make our peace with God, obtain His favor, and keep ourselves in His love. Therefore, no business for the world will serve to excuse us for not attending on God. On the contrary, the more important our worldly business, the more we need to pray to God for His blessing on it. By doing this, we will take Him along with us in our business. The closer we keep to prayer, and to God in prayer, the more all our affairs will prosper.

Should I prevail with you now to let God frequently hear from you? Let Him hear your voice, even if it is only the voice of your breathing, which is a sign of life. *"Thou hast heard my voice: hide not thine ear at my breathing, at my cry"* (Lam. 3:56). Let Him hear you, even if it is only the voice of your groanings, and those so weak that they cannot be uttered (Rom. 8:26). Speak to Him, even if it is in a broken language, as Hezekiah did: *"Like a crane or a swallow, so did I chatter"* (Isa. 38:14).

Speak often to Him; He is always within hearing. Hear Him speaking to you, and be mindful of His voice in everything you say to Him. Even as you lay a business letter before you when you write an answer to it, God's Word must be the guide of your desires and the ground of your expectations in prayer. You cannot expect Him to give a gracious ear to what you say to Him if you turn a deaf ear to what He says to you.

You see that you have frequent occasion to speak with God. Therefore, you do well to grow in your acquaintance with Him, to take heed to do nothing that would displease Him, and to strengthen your interest in the Lord Jesus through whom alone you have access with boldness to Him. Keep your voice in tune for prayer, and let all your language be a pure language that you may be fit to call on the name of the Lord.

In every prayer, remember that you are speaking to God, and show that you have an awe of Him within your spirit. Let us not be rash with our mouths or hasty to utter anything before God, but let every word be well weighed because God is in heaven, and we are on the earth (Eccl. 5:2). If He had not invited and encouraged us to do it, it would have been an unpardonable presumption for such sinful worms as we are to speak to the Lord of glory. And we do well to speak from the heart, heartily, for it is for our lives, and for the life of our souls, that we are speaking to Him.

Chapter 2

Directing Your Prayer to God

*In the morning will I direct my prayer
unto thee, and will look up.*
—Psalm 5:3

Not only must God hear our voices, but we must also with deliberation and design address ourselves to Him. We must direct our prayers unto God, as our text says: *"I* [will] *direct my prayer unto thee."* The original text contains no more than the words, "I will direct unto Thee." We could supply the words *my soul:* "I will direct my soul unto Thee." This would agree with Psalm 25:1: *"Unto thee, O Lord, do I lift up my soul."* Or, we could say, "I will direct my affections unto Thee"; in other words, "Having set my love upon You, I will let out my love to You." However, our translation very well supplies the words *my prayer:* *"I* [will] *direct my prayer unto thee."*

When I pray to You, I will direct my prayers. This denotes a fixedness of thought and an intent application of mind to the duty of prayer. We must go about it solemnly, as those who have something momentous on their hearts and on their minds, and therefore dare not trifle with it.

When we go to pray, we must not give the sacrifice of fools, who do not think about either what is to be done or what is to be gained. But we must speak the words of the wise, who aim at some good end in what they say and suit their words to that end. We must have in our eyes God's glory and our own true happiness. And the covenant of grace is so well ordered that God has been pleased therein to twist interests with us so that, in seeking His glory, we seek our own true interests, too.

This is directing the prayer, as he who shoots an arrow at a mark directs it and, with a fixed eye and steady hand, takes aim. This is engaging the heart to approach God and, in order to do so, disengaging it from everything else. He who takes aim with one eye, shuts the other. If we would direct a prayer to God, we must look away from all other things, must gather in our wandering thoughts, must summon them all to draw near and give their attendance, for here is work to be done that needs them all and is well worthy of them all. Thus we will be able to say with the psalmist, *"My heart is fixed, O God, my heart is fixed"* (Ps. 57:7).

When I direct my prayer, I will direct it to God and none other. Directing our prayers to God shows two things. First, it shows the sincerity of our habitual intention in prayer. We must not direct our prayers to men, so that we may gain praise and applause with them, as the Pharisees did. They proclaimed their devotions as they did their alms so that they might gain a reputation. Truly, Pharisees already have their reward; men commend them, but God abhors their pride and hypocrisy.

We must not let our prayers run at large, as they did who said, *"Who will show us any good?"* (Ps. 4:6). We must not direct them to the world, courting its smiles and pursuing its wealth, as those who do not cry unto God with their hearts because they *"assemble themselves for corn and wine"* (Hos. 7:14).

Let not self, carnal self, be the spring and center of your prayers, but God. Let this be the habitual disposition of your soul: to be to your God *"a name and a praise"* (Zeph. 3:20). Let this be your intention in all your desires, that God may be glorified; and by this let all your desires be directed, determined, sanctified, and, when need be, overruled.

Our Savior has plainly taught us this in the first petition of the Lord's Prayer: *"Hallowed be thy name"* (Matt. 6:9). Our purpose is to glorify His name, and other things are desired in order to accomplish that. It is because we seek the sanctification of His name that we desire His kingdom to come and His will to be done, and that we may be fed, kept, and pardoned. A habitual aim at God's glory is the sincerity that is our gospel perfection, the single eye that, where it is found, causes the whole body, the whole soul, to be full of light. Thus the prayer is directed to God.

Directing our prayers to God shows a second thing. It speaks of the steadiness of our actual regard to God in prayer. We must direct our prayers to God. We must direct our prayers as we direct our speech to the person we have business with. The Bible is a letter God has sent to us; prayer is a letter we send to Him. Now, you know it is essential to a letter that it be directed and vital that it be directed accurately. If it is not, it is in danger of miscarrying, which may cause problems. You pray daily and therein send letters to God; you do not know what you lose if your letters miscarry. Will you therefore take instructions on how to direct them to Him?

Give Him His titles, as you do when you direct a letter to a person of honor. Address Him as the great Jehovah, God over all, blessed forevermore; the King of Kings and Lord of Lords; the Lord God, gracious and merciful. Let your heart and mouth be filled with holy adorings and admirings of Him.

Concentrate on those titles of His that are proper to strike a holy awe of Him on your mind so that you may worship Him with reverence and godly fear. Direct your prayer to Him as the God of glory, with whom is terrible majesty and whose greatness is unsearchable, so that you may not dare to trifle with Him or to mock Him in what you say to Him.

Take notice of your relation to Him as His child, and do not let that be overlooked and lost in your awe-filled adorations of His glories. I have been told of a good man who kept a record of his experiences, which was found after his death. Among his recorded experiences was this one. One time, in secret prayer, his heart was at first much enlarged in giving to God those titles that are majestic and tremendous, in calling Him the great, the mighty, and the terrible God. But, going on thus, he checked himself with this thought: "And why not my Father?"

Christ has taught us, both by His precepts and by His example, to address ourselves to God as our Father. And the spirit of adoption teaches us to cry, *"Abba, Father"* (Rom. 8:15). A son, though a prodigal, when he returns and repents, may go to his father and say to him, "Father, I have sinned." Though he is no longer worthy to be called a son, yet with bold humility he may call him father. When Ephraim bemoaned himself as a calf unaccustomed to the yoke, God bemoaned him as a dear son, as a pleasant child (Jer. 31:18, 20). If God is not ashamed to acknowledge the relation, let us not be afraid to do so.

Direct your prayer to Him in heaven. This our Savior has taught us in the preface to the Lord's Prayer: *"Our Father which art in heaven"* (Matt. 6:9). Not that He is confined to the heavens, or as if the heaven of heavens could contain Him. But there He is said to have prepared His throne, not only His throne of government by which His kingdom rules over all, but His throne of grace to which we must, by faith, draw near. We must view Him as God in heaven, as opposed to the gods of the heathen, which dwelt in temples made with hands.

Heaven is a high place, and we must address Him as a God infinitely above us. Heaven is the fountain of light, and we must address Him as *"the Father of lights"* (James 1:17). Heaven is a vantage point, and we must see His eye upon us, from there beholding all the children of men. It is a place of purity, and we must in prayer view Him as a holy God and give thanks at the remembrance of His holiness. It is the firmament of His power, and we must depend on Him as one to whom power belongs. When our Lord Jesus prayed, He lifted up His eyes to heaven to show us where to expect the blessings we need.

Direct your letter to be left with the Lord Jesus, the only Mediator between God and man. It will certainly miscarry if it is not put into His hand. He is that other angel who adds much incense to the prayers of saints and, so perfumed, presents them to the Father. (See Revelation 8:3.) What we ask of the Father must be in His name; what we expect from the Father must be by His hand. For He is the High Priest of our profession, who is ordained for men, to offer their gifts (Heb. 5:1). Direct the letter to be left with Him, and He will deliver it with care and speed and will make your service acceptable.

George Herbert, in his poem called "The Bag," movingly described the wound in Christ's side as He was hanging on the cross. In this poem, Christ says the following to all believers as He is going to heaven:

> If you have any thing to send or write,
>   I have no bag, but here is room;
> Unto my Father's hands and sight,
>   Believe me, it shall safely come.
> That I shall mind what you impart,
> Look, you may put it near my heart.
>
> Or if hereafter any of my friends
>   Will use me in this kind, the door
> Shall still be open; what he sends
>   I will present, and something more,
> Not to his hurt: sighs will convey
> Any thing to me. Hark, despair, away.

I Will Look Up

If we are to direct our prayers to God, then we must look up. That is, we must look up in our prayers as those who speak to one above us, infinitely above us, the High and Holy One who inhabits eternity. We must look up as those who expect every good and perfect gift to come from above, from *"the Father of lights"* (James 1:17), as those who desire to enter into the holiest in prayer and to draw near with a true heart. With an eye of faith we must look above the world and everything in it; we must look beyond the things of time. What is this world, and all things here below, to one who knows how to put a due estimate on spiritual blessings and heavenly things?

The spirit of a man at death goes upward (Eccl. 3:21), for it returns to God who gave it. Therefore, being mindful of its Creator, it must in every prayer look upward toward its God, toward its home. Man's spirit must set its affections on things above (Col. 3:2), wherein it has laid up its treasure. Let us therefore in prayer, *"lift up our heart with our hands unto God in the heavens"* (Lam. 3:41). Long ago it was common in some churches for the minister to stir up the people to pray, saying, "Up with your heart." Unto You, O Lord, do we lift up our souls (Ps. 25:1).

Not only must we look up in our prayers, but we must also look up after our prayers. We should look up after we pray with an eye of satisfaction and pleasure. Looking up is a sign of cheerfulness, just as a downcast look is a melancholy one. Having by prayer made our requests of God, we must look up as those who are well pleased, and, with an entire confidence in His wisdom and goodness, patiently expect the outcome.

Hannah, when she had prayed, looked up, looked pleasant. She *"went her way, and did eat, and her countenance was no more sad"* (1 Sam. 1:18). Prayer eases the hearts of good Christians. When we have prayed, we should look up as those who, through grace, have found peace.

We must look up with observation after we pray to see what answers God gives to our prayers. We must look up as one who has shot an arrow looks after it to see how near it comes to the mark. We must look within ourselves and observe what the condition of our spirits is after we have been at prayer, how well satisfied we are in the will of God, and how well disposed we are to accommodate ourselves to it. We must look around us and observe how His providence works concerning us. Then, if our prayers are answered, we may return to give thanks; if not, we may remove what hinders and continue waiting.

Thus we must wait on our watchtower to see what God will say to us. We must be ready to hear it, expecting that God will give us an answer of peace and resolving that we will return no more to folly (Ps. 85:8). Thus we must keep up our communion with God, hoping that whenever we lift up our hearts to Him, He will lift up the light of His countenance upon us. Sometimes the answer is quick: *"While they are yet speaking, I will hear"* (Isa. 65:24), quicker than the reply to any of our letters; but if it is not, we must wait.

Let us therefore learn to direct our prayers and to look up; to be inward with God in every duty; to make heart-work of it, or we make nothing of it. Let us not worship in the outward court when we are commanded and encouraged to enter within the veil.

Chapter 3

Morning Prayers

In the morning...
—Psalm 5:3

The particular time fixed in our text for the good work of prayer is the morning. The psalmist seems to emphasize this, for he uses the phrase *"in the morning"* twice in Psalm 5:3. The psalmist did not mean that we should pray then only, but we should pray then to begin with. Let the morning be one of the times for prayer.

Under the law, we find that every morning a lamb was offered in sacrifice. Every morning the priests burned incense. The singers stood every morning to thank the Lord. Morning sacrifices were also instituted in Ezekiel's temple. These things are a clear indication that the spiritual sacrifices should be offered by the spiritual priests every morning, as consistently as morning comes. Every Christian should pray in secret, and every head of every family should pray with his family, morning by morning. There are many good reasons for praying in the morning, and these I will expound on.

The morning is the first part of the day, and it is fit that He who is first should have the first and be served first. Whatever you do, begin with God. The world had its beginning from Him; we had our beginning from Him; therefore, whatever we begin, we should take Him along with us in it. The days of our lives, as soon as the sun of reason rises in the soul, should be devoted to God and employed in His service. From the womb of the morning let Christ have the dew of your youth (Ps. 110:3). The firstfruits were always to be the Lord's, as well as the firstlings of the flock.

Through morning and evening prayer, we give glory to Him who is the Alpha and the Omega, the first and the last. We must begin and end the day, and begin and end the night, with Him who is the beginning and the end, the first cause, and the last end.

Wisdom has said, *"Those that seek me early shall find me"* (Prov. 8:17)—that is, early in their lives and early in the day. For by seeking God early, we give to Him that which He ought to have:

the preference above all. Hereby we show that we seek Him diligently and that we are careful to please Him. What we do earnestly, we are told in Scripture to do early. Industrious men rise early. David expressed the strength and warmth of his devotion when he said, *"O God, thou art my God; early will I seek thee"* (Ps. 63:1).

Another good reason to pray in the morning is that we are fresh and alert and in the best condition. Then our spirits are revived with the rest and sleep of the night, and we live a kind of new life; the fatigues of the day before are forgotten. The God of Israel neither slumbers nor sleeps, yet, when He exerts Himself more than ordinary on His people's behalf, He is said to awake *"as one out of sleep"* (Ps. 78:65).

If we are ever good for anything, it is in the morning; it has therefore become a proverb, "The morning is a friend to the muses." If the morning is a friend to the muses, I am sure it is no less so to the graces. As He who is the first should have the first, so He who is the best should have the best. When we are fittest for business, we should apply ourselves to the most necessary business, which is prayer.

Worshiping God is work that requires the best powers of the soul, and it well deserves them. How can they be better bestowed? "[Let] *all that is within me, bless his holy name"* (Ps. 103:1), said

David, and all is little enough. If there is any gift in us by which God may be honored, the morning is the time to stir it up, when our spirits are refreshed and have gained new vigor. David stirred up his gift in the morning: *"Awake up, my glory; awake, psaltery and harp: I myself will awake early"* (Ps. 57:8). In the morning, let us stir ourselves up to take hold of God.

We should pray in the morning because we are then the freest from company and business. Ordinarily, the morning is the best opportunity for solitude and privacy, unless we are one of those sluggards who lie in bed saying, *"Yet a little sleep, a little slumber"* (Prov. 6:10) until the work of our calling calls us up with, *"How long wilt thou sleep, O sluggard?"* (Prov. 6:9). It is wise for those who have so much to do in the world that they have scarcely a minute to themselves all day to take time in the morning for the business of their religion before other business crowds in on them. In the morning they can be fully devoted to prayer and therefore the more intent on prayer.

As we should worship God when we are least burdened with deadness and dullness within, so also should we worship Him when we are least exposed to distraction and diversion without. The apostle suggests how careful we should be to *"attend upon the Lord without distraction"* (1 Cor. 7:35). Therefore, Sunday, the one day in seven that is appointed for holy work (the day that is the first day, too—the morning of the week), is appointed to be a day of rest from other work. Abraham left all at the bottom of the hill when he went up to the mountain to worship God.

In the morning therefore let us converse with God and apply ourselves to the concerns of the other life before we are entangled in the affairs of this life. Our Lord Jesus set us an example of this. Because His day was wholly filled up with public business for God and the souls of men, He rose up in the morning long before daybreak, and before company came in, and went to a solitary place and there prayed (Mark 1:35).

In the morning, we have received fresh mercies from God, which we should acknowledge with thankfulness to His praise. He is continually doing us good and loading us with His benefits. Every day we have reason to bless Him, for every day He is blessing us, particularly in the morning. He gives us the fruits of His favor, which are said to be new every morning (Lam. 3:22–23), because, though we had the same the morning before, they are still forfeited and are still needed, and on that account may still be called new. Therefore, as He is giving us the fruits of His favor every morning, we should still be returning the expressions of our gratitude to Him and expressions of other pious and devout affections, which, like the fire on the altar, must be new every morning.

Have we had a good night? Then do we not have an errand to the throne of grace to return thanks for it? Many mercies worked together to make it a good night! They were distinguishing mercies granted to us but denied to others. Many do not have a place to lay their heads; our Master Himself did not. *"The foxes have holes, and the birds of the air have nests; but the Son of man hath not where to lay his head"* (Matt. 8:20).

But we have houses to dwell in, quiet and peaceable habitations, perhaps stately ones. We have beds to lie in, warm and soft ones, perhaps beds of ivory, fine ones, like the ones those who were at ease in Zion stretched themselves out on. We are not forced to wander in deserts and mountains, in dens and caves of the earth, as some of the best of God's saints, of whom the world was not worthy, have been forced to do (Heb. 11:38).

Many have beds to lie on, yet dare not or cannot lie down on them, being kept up either by the sickness of their friends or the fear of their enemies. But we have lain down, and there has been no one to make us afraid and no threat of the sword, either of war or persecution.

Many lie down and cannot sleep but are full of tossings to and fro until the dawning of the day, through pain of body or anguish of mind. Wearisome nights are appointed to them, and their eyes are kept open. But we have lain down and slept without any disturbance, and our sleep has been sweet and refreshing, the pleasant parenthesis of our cares and toils. It is God who has given us sleep, has given it to us as He gives it to His beloved (Ps. 127:2).

Many lie down and sleep and never rise again; they sleep the sleep of death, and their beds are their graves. But we have slept and awakened again, have rested and are refreshed. We shake ourselves, and we awake as at other times, because the Lord has sustained us (Ps. 3:5). If He had not upheld us, we would have sunk with our own weight when we fell asleep.

Is it a pleasant morning? Is the light sweet to us? The light of the sun, the light of the eyes—do these rejoice the heart? Should we not acknowledge our obligations to Him who opens our eyes and opens the eyelids of the morning upon us?

Do we have clothes to put on in the morning, garments that warm us? Do we have a change of clothes, not for necessity only, but for ornament? Our clothes are from God; it is His wool and His flax that are given to cover us. And the morning when we dress ourselves is the proper time for giving Him thanks for our clothes. Yet, I fear, we do not thank God for our clothes as consistently as we give thanks for our food when we sit down to eat, though we have as much reason to do so.

Are we in health and at ease? Have we been so for a long time? We ought to be as thankful for a constant series of mercies as for particular instances of them, especially considering how many are sick and in pain and how much we have deserved to be so.

Perhaps we have experienced some special mercy to ourselves or our families, in preservation from fire or thieves, from dangers we have been aware of and many more unseen. Weeping, perhaps, endured for a night, but joy came in the morning (Ps. 30:5), and that calls aloud for us to acknowledge the goodness of God.

The destroying angel, perhaps, has been abroad, and the arrow that flies at midnight and destroys in darkness has been shot into the windows of others, but our houses have been passed over. Thanks be to God for the blood of the covenant, sprinkled on our doorposts! And thanks for the ministration of the good angels around us, to which we owe our preservation from the malice of the evil angels against us. I am speaking of those rulers of the darkness of the world, who, perhaps, creep forth like the beasts of prey when God brings darkness. All the glory be to the God of the angels!

We should pray in the morning because then we have fresh reasons given to us for the adoration of the greatness and glory of God. We ought to take notice of the gifts of God's bounty to us, of which we have the comfort and benefit. But little, narrow souls confine their regards to them. We ought to also observe the more general instances of His wisdom and power in the kingdom of providence, which overflow to His honor and the common good of the universe.

The nineteenth Psalm seems to have been a morning meditation. It directs us to observe how *"the heavens declare the glory of God; and the firmament showeth his handiwork"* (v. 1). We should acknowledge not only the advantage we receive from their light and influence, but also the honor they do to Him *"who stretch*[ed] *out the heavens like a curtain"* (Ps. 104:2), fixed their pillars, and established their ordinances. According to these ordinances, they continue to this day, for they are all His servants (Ps. 119:91).

Day unto day utters this speech, and night unto night shows His knowledge (Ps. 19:2), even the eternal power and Godhead of the great Creator and Ruler of the world. The constant succession of light and darkness, according to the original contract made between them, that they should reign alternately, may serve to confirm our faith in the biblical account of Creation and in the promise of God after the Flood:

While the earth remaineth, seedtime and harvest, and cold and heat, and summer

> *and winter, and day and night shall not cease.* (Gen. 8:22)

Jeremiah 33:20 speaks of His *"covenant of the day, and...of the night."*

Look up in the morning, and see how exactly the dayspring knows its place, knows its time, and keeps them. See how the morning light takes hold of the ends of the earth and of the air, which is turned to it as clay to the seal, instantly receiving the impressions of it (Job 38:12–14).

A good and worthy minister recently expressed this idea in a way that pleased me very much. During his thanksgivings to God for the mercies of the morning, he said, "How many thousand miles has the sun traveled this last night to bring the light of the morning to us poor, sinful wretches, who justly might have been buried in the darkness of the night!"

Look up and see the sun as a bridegroom richly dressed and greatly pleased, coming out of his chamber, and as a strong man rejoicing to run a race (Ps. 19:4–5). Observe how bright its beams are, how sweet its smiles, how strong its influences.

"There is no speech nor language, where their voice is not heard" (Ps. 19:3), that is, the voice of the heavens—those natural preachers who proclaim the glory of God. Since this is so, it is a pity

there should be any speech or language where the voices of God's worshipers should not be heard. Our voices should echo the voices of those natural preachers and ascribe glory to Him who makes *"the morning and evening to rejoice"* (Ps. 65:8). Whatever others do, let Him hear our voices to this purpose in the morning. Let us direct our praises unto Him in the morning.

In the morning, we have, or should have, fresh thoughts of God and sweet meditations on His name—and those we ought to offer up to Him in prayer. Have we been, according to David's example, remembering God upon our beds and meditating on Him in the night watches (Ps. 63:6)? When we awake, can we say as he did, that we are still with God (Ps. 139:18)? If so, we have a good errand to the throne of grace, by way of the words of our mouths, to offer up to God the meditations of our hearts. They will be to Him a sweet-smelling sacrifice. If the heart has been overflowing with a good matter, let the tongue be like the pen of a ready writer, pouring it out before God (Ps. 45:1).

We have the Word of God to become acquainted with, and we ought to read a portion of it every morning. By it God speaks to us, and in it we ought to meditate day and night. If we do meditate in His Word, that will send us to the throne of grace and furnish us with many a good errand there. If God in the morning, by His grace, directs His Word to us so as to make it reach our hearts, that will engage us to direct our prayers to Him.

In the morning, we often reflect upon many vain and sinful thoughts that have been in our minds in the night season, and for that reason it is necessary to pray to God in the morning for the pardon of them. The Lord's Prayer seems to be calculated primarily for the morning, for we are taught to pray for our daily bread at the beginning of each day. Yet we are then to pray, "Father, forgive us our trespasses" (Matt. 6:12); for just as we contract guilt in the hurry of the day by our irregular words and actions, so we do in the solitude of the night by our corrupt imaginations and the wanderings of an unsanctified, ungoverned fancy.

It is certain that *"the thought of foolishness is sin"* (Prov. 24:9). Foolish thoughts are sinful thoughts—the firstborn of the old man, the first beginnings of all sin. How many of these vain thoughts lodge within us wherever we lodge! Their name is Legion, for they are many. Who can understand these errors? They are more than the hairs on our heads.

We read of those who *"work evil upon their beds,"* because there they devise it, and *"when the morning is light, they practice it"* (Mic. 2:1). In the night season, the mind is often disquieted and distracted with distrustful, anxious thoughts; polluted with unchaste and wanton thoughts;

intoxicated with proud, aspiring thoughts; soured and leavened with malicious, revengeful thoughts; or, at the best, diverted from devout and pious thoughts by a thousand trifles.

Out of the heart proceed evil thoughts that lie down with us and rise up with us. For out of this corrupt fountain, which, of course, we carry with us wherever we go, these streams naturally flow. Yes, and in the multitude of dreams, as well as in many words, there are also various vanities (Eccl. 5:7).

And do we dare go anywhere until we have renewed our repentance? We are every night, as well as every day, committing sins. Should we not confess to Him, who knows our hearts, their wanderings from Him? Should we not complain of them to Him as revolting and rebellious hearts, tending to backslide? Should we not make our peace with the blood of Christ and pray so that the thoughts of our hearts may be forgiven us (Acts 8:22)? We cannot safely go into the business of the day under the guilt of any sin unrepented of or unpardoned.

In the morning, we are getting ready for the work of the day; therefore, we should seek God, by prayer, for His presence and blessing. We come, and are encouraged to come boldly, to the throne of grace, not only for mercy to pardon what has been amiss but also for grace to help in every time of need (Heb. 4:16). What time is not a time of need for us? Therefore, what morning should pass without morning prayer? We read in Ezra 3:4 about the offerings that were required every day. And, in reference to that, we must go to God every morning to pray for the gracious disposal of His providence concerning us and the gracious operations of His Spirit upon us.

Perhaps you have a family to look after and to provide for, and you are concerned about doing well for them. Then, every morning, by prayer, commit them to God. If you put them under the guidance and government of His grace, you effectually put them under the care and protection of His providence. Job rose up early in the morning to offer burnt offerings for his children, and we should rise up early to offer prayers and supplications for our children, even *according to the number of them all* (Job 1:5). In this way we cause the blessing to rest on our homes.

Perhaps you are going about the business of your callings. Look up to God, then, in the first place for wisdom and grace to manage them well, in the fear of God, and second, to abide with Him in them. Then you may entreat Him in faith to prosper you in them, to strengthen you for the services of them, to support you under the fatigues of them, to direct the designs of them, and to give you comfort in the gains of them.

Perhaps you have a journey to go on. Look up to God for His presence with you, and go no place where you cannot, in faith, entreat God to go with you.

You have opportunities, perhaps, of doing or getting good. Look up to God so that you may have heart for every opportunity in your hands. Look to God for skill and will and courage to improve the opportunity, so that it is not a price in the hand of a fool. (See Proverbs 17:16.) Every day has its temptations, too; some, perhaps, you foresee, but there may be many more that you do not think of. You should therefore be earnest with God so that you may not be led into any temptation but instead guarded against all of them. You should entreat God so that you may have wisdom, in whatever company you find yourself in, to do good and not harm to them and to get good and not harm by them.

We do not know what a day may bring forth (Prov. 27:1). Few of us think in the morning about what tidings we may hear or what events may befall us before night. We should beg God for grace to carry us through the duties and difficulties that we do not foresee as well as those that we do. In order that we may stand *"complete in all the will of God"* (Col. 4:12), we should pray that as the day is, so our strength may be (Deut. 33:25). We will find that *"sufficient unto the day is the evil thereof"* (Matt. 6:34), and that therefore as it is folly to think about tomorrow's event, so it is wisdom to think about today's duty. The supplies of divine grace are sufficient for this day and the duty of it. We should pray that God's grace will thoroughly furnish us for every good word and work and thoroughly fortify us against every evil word and work, that God's grace will help us not to think, speak, or do anything all day that we will wish unthought, unspoken, or undone at night.

Consistent Secret Worship

May our text, Psalm 5:3, make us aware of our omissions, for omissions are sins and must come into judgment. How often our morning worship has been either neglected or negligently performed! The work has been either not done at all or done deceitfully; either not a sacrifice at all or a sacrifice that is torn, lame, or sick; either no prayer or a prayer not directed properly, nor lifted up. We have had the morning's mercies; God has not been lacking in the compassion and care of a father toward us. Yet we have not done the morning's service but have been shamefully lacking in the duty of children toward Him.

Let us be truly humbled before God for our sins and follies herein, that we have so often robbed God of the honor, and ourselves of the benefit, of our morning worship. God has come into our prayer closets seeking this fruit but has found none, or next to none. He has listened, but either we did not speak to Him at all, or did not speak what was right. Some trifling thing or other has served for an excuse to neglect our morning worship once; and when once the good practice has been disrupted, conscience has been wounded and its bonds have been weakened. We have grown more and more negligent of our morning worship, and perhaps by degrees we have quite given it up.

I entreat you, receive a word of exhortation concerning this. How great an influence it would have upon the prosperity of your soul to be constant and sincere in your secret worship! Therefore, allow me to press it upon you with all earnestness. Let God hear from you every morning; every morning let your prayer be directed to Him, and look up.

Be conscientious in this matter of secret worship. Keep it up, not only because it has been a custom you have received by tradition from your fathers, but because it is a duty, concerning which you have received commandments from the Lord. Keep up stated times for it, and be true to them. Let those who have lived up to this point in the total neglect or the frequent omission of secret prayer, be persuaded from this point forward to look on it as the most necessary part of daily business and the most delightful part of daily comfort. May they do it accordingly with constant care and, yet, with constant pleasure.

No one who has use of his reason can pretend to have an exemption from this duty. What is said to some is said to all: "Pray, pray! *'Continue in prayer, and watch in the same'* (Col. 4:2)." Rich people are not so much bound to labor with their hands as the poor; poor people are not so much bound to give alms as the rich; but both are equally bound to pray. The rich are not above the necessity of the duty, nor the poor below acceptance with God in it. It is not too soon for the youngest to begin to pray. And those to whom the multitude of years has taught wisdom will be fools if they think, at their end, they have no further occasion for prayer.

Let no one insist that he cannot pray, for if you were ready to perish with hunger, you could beg and pray for food. Likewise, if you see yourself ruined because of sin, can you not beg and pray for mercy and grace? Are you a Christian? If so, never out of shame say, "I cannot pray," for that is as absurd as a soldier saying he does not know how to handle a sword, or a carpenter a saw. Why are you called into the fellowship of Christ, except that by Him you may have fellowship with God? Even if you cannot pray as well as others, pray as well as you can, and God will accept your prayers.

Let no one plead that he does not have time in the morning for prayer. I dare say that you can find time for other things that are less needful; it would be better to take time from sleep than to lack time for prayer. How can you spend time better and more to your satisfaction and advantage? All the business of the day will prosper the better if you begin it in prayer with God.

Let none plead that he does not have a convenient place to privately pray. Isaac retired into the field to pray. The psalmist could be alone with God in the corner of a housetop. If you cannot pray with as much secrecy as you would like, pray anyway. It is doing it with ostentation that is wrong, not doing it under observation when it cannot be avoided.

I remember when I was a young man going up to London in the stagecoach in King James's time. There happened to be a gentleman in the company who was not afraid to say he was a Jesuit. Many a conflict he and I had on the trip, and this was one: He was praising the custom in certain countries of keeping the church doors always open for people to go in at any time to say their prayers. I told him this practice was too much like that of the Pharisees, who prayed in the synagogues, and that it did not agree with Christ's command: *"Thou, when thou prayest, enter into thy closet, and…shut thy door"* (Matt. 6:6), not "go into the church with the doors open."

When he was pressed with that argument, he replied with some vehemence, "I believe you Protestants say your prayers nowhere; for I have traveled a great deal in the coach in company with Protestants, and have often slept in inns in the same room with them, and have carefully watched them, and could never perceive that any of them said his prayers, night or morning, but one, and he was a Presbyterian." I hope there was more malice than truth in what he said; but I mention it as a lesson, that though we cannot be as private as we would like in our devotions, yet we must not omit them, lest the omission should prove not only a sin, but a scandal.

Make a business of your secret worship, and do not be slothful in this business, but *"fervent in spirit; serving the Lord"* (Rom. 12:11). Take heed lest it degenerate into a formality and you grow customary in your accustomed services. Go about the duty solemnly; be inward with God in it. It is not enough to say your prayers, but you must earnestly pray your prayers as Elijah did. Let us learn to labor fervently in prayer as Epaphras did. We will find that it is the hand of the diligent in this duty that makes rich (Prov. 10:4). God does not look at the length of your prayers, nor will you be heard for your fine speaking, or *"much speaking"* (Matt. 6:7). God requires *"truth in the inward parts"* (Ps. 51:6), and it is the prayer of the upright that is His delight (Prov. 15:8).

When you have prayed, consider yourself encouraged, both to serve God and to trust in Him, so that the comfort and benefit of your morning devotions may not be like the morning cloud that passes away, but like the morning light that shines more and more.

Chapter 4

Spending the Day with God

On thee do I wait all the day.
—Psalm 25:5

Which of us can truly say that he waits on God all the day? Who lives this life of communion with God, which is so much our business and so much our blessedness? How far short do we come of the spirit of David, though we have much better helps for our acquaintance with God than the saints then had? For we have the clearer discoveries of the mediation of Christ.

Yet, so that weak Christians who are sincere may not despair, let us remember that David himself was not always in such a condition that he could say that he waited on God all the day. He had his infirmities, and yet he was a man after

God's own heart. We have our infirmities, but if they are sincerely lamented and striven against, and if the habitual bent of our souls is toward God and heaven, we will be accepted through Christ, for we are *"not under the law, but under grace"* (Rom. 6:14).

However, David's statement in the text shows us what our practice should be: On God we must wait all the day. That denotes two things: a patient expectation and a constant attendance.

A Patient Expectation

Our text speaks of a patient expectation of His coming to us in a way of mercy. For this first meaning, *"all the day"* must be taken figuratively, meaning all the time that the desired mercy is delayed.

David, in the former part of the verse, prayed for divine guidance and instruction: *"Lead me in thy truth, and teach me"* (Ps. 25:5). He was at a loss. He was very eager to know what God would have him to do and was ready to do it, but God kept him in suspense. He was not yet sure about the mind and will of God, about what he should do or what course he should steer.

Will he therefore proceed without divine direction? No. *"On thee* [will] *I wait all the day"* (Ps. 25:5). He waited, even as we see Abraham waiting in Genesis 15:8–21. Abraham attended upon the sacrifice from morning until sundown before God gave him an answer to his inquiries concerning his seed. David waited, even as Habakkuk stood on his watchtower to see what answer God would give him when he consulted His oracle; and, though the answer does not come at once, *"at the end it shall speak, and not lie"* (Hab. 2:3).

David, in the words before the text, had called God the God of his salvation (Ps. 25:5), the God on whom he depended for salvation, both temporal and eternal. From God he expected deliverance out of his present distresses, those troubles of his heart that were enlarged (v. 17), and out of the hands of those enemies who were ready to triumph over him (v. 2), those who hated him with a cruel hatred (v. 19). Hoping that God would be his Savior, he resolved to wait on Him all the day, like a genuine son of Jacob, whose dying statement was, *"I have waited for thy salvation, O LORD"* (Gen. 49:18).

Sometimes God precedes His people with the blessings of His goodness; before they call, He answers them (Isa. 65:24). He is in the midst of His church, to *"help her, and that right early"* (Ps. 46:5). But at other times, He seems to stand far away; He delays the deliverance and keeps them long in expectation of it—no, in suspense about it. It is a cloudy and dark day, and it is not until evening that it is light, that the comfort comes that they have been kept waiting for all day. No, perhaps it does not come until far in the night; it is at midnight that the cry is made, *"Behold, the bridegroom cometh"* (Matt. 25:6).

The deliverance of the church out of her troubles, the success of her struggles and rest from them, the rescue from under the rod of the wicked, and the accomplishment of all that God has promised concerning the church—these are what we must continue humbly waiting on God for, without distrust or impatience. We must wait all the day.

Though it is a long day, though we are kept waiting a great while, quite beyond our own estimations, we are still obliged to wait longer. We are bid with Elijah's servant to go seven times before we perceive the least sign of mercy coming. We thought that this and the other had been he who should have delivered Israel, but are disappointed.

"The harvest is past, the summer is ended, and we are not saved" (Jer. 8:20). The time is prolonged; no, the opportunities are neglected. The summer time, and harvest time, when we thought we would reap the fruit of all our prayers and pains and patience, is past and ended, and we are as far as ever from salvation.

The time that the ark abode in Kirjathjearim was long, much longer than the people thought it would be when it was first lodged there. *"It was twenty years: and all the house of Israel lamented after the LORD"* (1 Sam. 7:2). They began to fear it would abide forever in that obscurity.

But though it is a long day, it is only a day, only one day, and it is known to the Lord (Zech. 14:7). The time that we are kept waiting seems long, but the happy result will enable us to reflect upon the time as short, as but a moment. It is no longer than God has appointed, and we are sure His time is the best time and His favors are worth waiting for. The time is long, but it is nothing compared with the days of eternity, when those who had great patience will be recompensed for it with an everlasting salvation.

Though it is a dark day, let us wait on God all the day. Even though, while we are kept waiting for what God will do, we are kept in the dark concerning what He is doing and what is best for us to do, let us be content to wait in the dark. Though we do not see any signs, though there is no one to tell us how long, let us resolve to wait, however long it may be. For, though we do not know right now what God is doing, we will know hereafter, when the mystery of God is finished.

Never was man more at a loss concerning God's dealings with him than poor Job was. He said,

> *I go forward, but he is not there; and backward, but I cannot perceive him: on the left hand...on the right hand,* [but] *I cannot see him.* (Job 23:8–9)

Yet he sat down, resolving to wait on God all the day with a satisfaction in this: though I do not know the way that He takes, *"he knoweth the way that I take: when he hath tried me, I shall come forth as gold"* (Job 23:10). Like refined gold, I will be approved and improved. God sits by as a refiner and will take care that the gold is in the furnace no longer than is necessary for the refining of it. Even when God's way is in the sea so that He cannot be traced (Ps. 77:19), we are sure His way is in the sanctuary (Ps. 77:13) so that He can be trusted. And when clouds and darkness are round about Him, even then justice and judgment *"are the habitation of his throne"* (Ps. 97:2).

Though it is a stormy day, we must wait on God all the day. Though the wind not only fails to drive us forward, but is contrary and drives us back; though it is boisterous, and the church is tossed with tempests and ready to sink, we must hope for the best. We must wait and weather the storm by patience. It is a comfort that Christ is in the ship. The church's cause is Christ's cause; He has embraced it, and He will own it. He is in the same vessel with His people. Why, then, are you fearful? Have no doubt that the ship will come safely to land. Though Christ seems for the present to be asleep, the prayers of His disciples will awaken Him, and He will rebuke the winds and the waves. Though the bush burn, if God is in it, it will not be consumed.

Yet this is not all. Christ is not only in the ship, but also at the helm. Whatever threatens the church is ordered by the Lord Jesus and will be made to work for its good. This idea is excellently expressed by George Herbert:

> Away despair, my gracious God doth hear,
> When winds and waves assault my keel,
> He doth preserve it, he doth steer,
> E'en when the boat seems most to reel.
> Storms are the triumph of his art,
> Well may he close his eyes, but not his heart.

It is a seasonable word for this day. What God will do with us we cannot tell; but this we are sure of, that He is a God of judgment, infinitely wise and just, and therefore *"Blessed are all they that wait for him"* (Isa. 30:18). He will do His own work in His own way and time. Though we are hurried back into the wilderness when we thought we were about to enter Canaan, we suffer justly for our unbelief and murmurings. But God acts wisely and will be found faithful to His promise. His time to judge for His people and to have compassion on His servants is when He sees that their strength is gone (Deut. 32:36). This was seen of old in the mount of the Lord and will be again. Therefore, let us continue in a waiting attitude. Hold onto faith and patience, for it is good that a man should both hope and wait quietly for the salvation of the Lord.

Experiencing God's Presence

A Constant Attendance

Our text, *"On thee do I wait all the day,"* also speaks of a constant attendance upon God in a way of duty. And so, in this case, we can take *"the day"* literally. It was David's practice to wait on God all the day. The word signifies both every day and all the day long; it is the same with that command, *"Be thou in the fear of the LORD all the day long"* (Prov. 23:17).

For the explanation of this, I must show what it means to wait on God. Then I will show that it is not enough for us to begin every day with God; we must wait on Him every day and all the day long.

Let us find out what it means to wait on God. You have read how much it is our duty in the morning to speak to Him in solemn prayer. But are we then done with Him for the day? No, we must still wait on Him, as one to whom we are very closely related and very greatly indebted. To wait on God is to live a life of desire toward Him, delight in Him, dependence on Him, and devotion to Him.

Waiting on God is living a life of desire toward God. It means to wait on Him as the beggar waits on his benefactor, with earnest desire to receive supplies from him. It means to wait as the sick and sore at Bethesda's pool waited for the stirring of the water and stayed on the porches with desire to be helped in and healed. When the prophet said, *"In the way of thy judgments, O LORD, have we waited for thee,"* he explained himself in the next words: *"The desire of our soul is to thy name, and to the remembrance of thee. With my soul have I desired thee"* (Isa. 26:8–9).

Our desire must be not only toward the good things that God gives, but toward God Himself, His favor and love, the manifestation of His name to us, and the influence of His grace upon us. We wait on God when our souls pant after Him and His favor, when we thirst for God, for the living God. Oh, that I may behold the beauty of the Lord! Oh, that I may taste His goodness! Oh, that I may bear His image and be entirely conformed to His will! For there is none in heaven or earth that I can desire in comparison with Him. Oh, that I may know Him more, love Him better, be brought nearer to Him, and be made fitter for Him. Thus, upon the wings of holy desire, our souls should still be soaring upward toward God, still pressing forward, forward toward heaven.

We must not only pray solemnly in the morning, but that desire which is the life and soul of prayer, like the fire upon the altar, must be kept continually burning, ready for the sacrifices that are to be offered upon it. The bent and bias of the soul in all its internal workings must be toward God—the serving of Him in all we do and the enjoying of Him in all we have. This is principally intended in the commands given us to *"pray always"* (Luke 21:36), to *"pray without ceasing"* (1 Thess. 5:17), to *"continue in prayer"* (Col. 4:2). Even when we are not making actual addresses to God, we must have habitual inclinations toward Him. A man in health, though he is not always eating, always has a disposition in him toward the nourishment and delights of the body. In this way we must always be waiting on God, as our chief good, and moving toward Him.

To wait on God is to live a life of delight in God, as the lover waits on his beloved. Desire is love in motion, like a bird upon his wing; delight is love at rest, like a bird upon the nest. Though our desire must still be so toward God that we wish for more of God, our delight must be so in God that we never wish for more than God. Believing Him to be a God all-sufficient, in Him we must be entirely satisfied. Let Him be mine, and I have enough. Do we love to love God? Is it a pleasure to us to think that there is a God? Is it a pleasure that He is such a one as He has revealed Himself to be? Is it a pleasure that He is our God by Creation to direct us as He pleases, our God in covenant to direct all circumstances for our best? This is waiting on our God, always looking up to Him with pleasure.

There is something or other the soul has that it values itself by, something or other that it reposes itself in. What is it? God or the world? What is it that we pride ourselves in, that we make the matter of our boasting? It is the character of worldly people to *"boast themselves in the multitude of their riches"* (Ps. 49:6) and to boast of their own might and the power of their own hands, which they think have gotten them their wealth. It is the character of godly people to boast in God *"all the day long"* (Ps. 44:8). That is waiting on God: having our eyes always on Him with a secret satisfaction, as men have on that which is their glory and that which they glory in.

What is it that we please ourselves with, that we embrace with the greatest satisfaction? The worldly man, when his barns are full of corn, says, *"Soul...take thine ease, eat, drink, and be merry"* (Luke 12:19). The godly man can never say so until he finds his heart full of God and Christ and grace; only then does he say, *"'Return unto thy rest, O my soul'* (Ps. 116:7), here repose yourself." The gracious soul dwells in God, is at home in Him, and there dwells at ease. In Him, he is perpetually pleased. Whatever he meets with in the world to make himself uneasy, he finds enough in God to balance it.

To wait on God is to live a life of dependence on God, as a child who has confidence in his father waits on him and casts on him all his care. To wait on God is to expect all good to come to us from Him, as the worker of all good for us and in us, the giver of all good to us, and the protector of us from all evil. Thus David explained himself: *"My soul, wait thou only upon God* [and continue still to do so]*; for my expectation is from him"* (Ps. 62:5). I do not look to anyone else for the good I need; for I know that every creature is what God makes him to be to me, and no more, and every man's judgment proceeds from God.

Should we lift up our eyes to the hills? Does our help come from there? Does the dew that waters the valleys come from a place no higher than the tops of the hills? Should we go higher and lift up our eyes to the heavens, to the clouds? Can they of themselves give rain? No, if God does not hear the heavens, they do not hear the earth. We must therefore look above the hills, above the heavens, for all our help comes from the Lord. This was the acknowledgment of a king, and not a good king either: *"If the LORD do not help thee, whence shall I help thee? out of the barnfloor, or out of the winepress?"* (2 Kings 6:27).

Our expectations from God, as far as they are guided by and grounded on the word that He has spoken, ought to be humbly confident and with a full assurance of faith. We must know and be sure that no word of God will fall to the ground, that *"the expectation of the poor shall not perish"* (Ps. 9:18). Worldly people say to their gold, "You are my hope," and to the fine gold, *"Thou art my confidence"* (Job 31:24). *"The rich man's wealth is his strong city"* (Prov. 10:15). But God is the only refuge and portion of the godly man here in the land of the living. It is to God only that he says (and he says it with a holy boldness), "You are my hope and my confidence."

The eyes of all things wait on Him (Ps. 145:15), for He is good to all; but the eyes of His saints wait especially, for He is in a special manner good to Israel. They know His name and therefore will trust and triumph in Him as those who know they will not be made ashamed of their hope.

To wait on God is to live a life of devotion to God as the servant waits on his master, ready to observe his will and to do his work and in everything to consult his honor and interest. To wait on God is to entirely and unreservedly refer ourselves to His wise and holy directions and arrangements and to cheerfully acquiesce in them and comply with them. The servant who waits on his master does not choose his own way, but follows his master step by step. In the same way we must wait on God as those who have no wills of their own, except what is wholly resolved into His, and must therefore study to accommodate themselves to His. It is the character of the redeemed of the Lord, that they follow the Lamb wherever He goes (Rev. 14:4) with an implicit faith and obedience. As the eyes of a servant are on the hand of his master and the eyes of a maiden on the hand of her mistress, so must our eyes wait on the Lord to do what He appoints us, to take what He allots us. Our attitude should be, "Father, Your will be done; Master, Your will be done."

The servant waits on his master, not only to do him service but also to do him honor. Thus we must wait on God, so that we may be to Him *"for a name, and for a praise"* (Jer. 13:11). His glory must be our ultimate end to which we—and all we are, have, and can do—must be dedicated. We wear His uniform, attend in His courts, and follow His directions as His servants for this purpose, that He may in all things be glorified.

To wait on God is to make His will our rule. It means to make the will of His precept the rule of our practice, and to do every duty with that in mind. We must wait on Him to receive His commands, with a resolution to comply with them, regardless of how much they may contradict our corrupt inclinations or secular interests. We must wait on Him as the holy angels do who always behold the face of the Father, as those who are at His beck and call and are ready to go upon the least indication of His will, wherever He sends them. Thus we must do the will of God, as the angels do it who are in heaven, those ministers of His that are always about His throne in order to do His pleasure.

Spending the Day with God

David prayed in Psalm 25:5 that God would show him His way and lead him, teach him, keep him, and forward him in the way of his duty. So the text comes in as a plea to enforce that petition, for *"on thee do I wait all the day,"* ready to receive the law from Your mouth and in everything to observe Your orders. Then the text indicates this, that those, and only those who are ready and willing to do as they are taught, can expect to be taught by God. If any man will do His will and is steadfastly resolved in the strength of His grace to comply with it, he will know what His will is. David prayed, *"Give me understanding,"* and then promised himself, *"I shall keep thy law; yea, I shall observe it"* (Ps. 119:34), as the servant who waits on his master.

Those who go up to the house of the Lord with an expectation that He will teach them His ways must go with a humble resolution that they will walk in His paths (Isa. 2:3). Lord, let the pillar of cloud and fire go before me, for I am determined with full purpose of heart to follow it and thus to wait on my God all the day.

To wait on God is to make the will of His providence the rule of our patience and to bear every affliction with our focus on that. We are sure it is God who performs all things for us (Ps. 57:2), and He performs the things that are appointed for us. We are just as sure that all God does is well, and it will be made to work for good to all who love Him

(Rom. 8:28). Therefore, we ought to acquiesce in, and accommodate ourselves to, the whole will of God.

To wait on the Lord is to say, *"It is the LORD: let him do* [to me] *what seemeth him good"* (1 Sam. 3:18), because nothing seems good to Him but what really is good, and this we will see when God's work appears in a full light. To wait on God is to say, *"'Not as I will, but as thou wilt'* (Matt. 26:39), for should things be according to my mind?" It is to reconcile our minds to our conditions in everything so as to keep them calm and easy, regardless of what happens to make us uneasy. We must therefore bear the affliction, whatever it is, because it is the will of God. It is what He has allotted us, and He does all things according to the counsel of His own will.

This is Christian patience: *"I was dumb, I opened not my mouth,"* not because it was to no purpose to complain, but *"because thou didst it"* (Ps. 39:9), and therefore I had no reason to complain. And this will reconcile us to every affliction, one as well as another, because whatever it is, it is the will of God.

In compliance with it, we must not only be silent because of the sovereignty of His will—*"Woe unto him that striveth with his Maker!"* (Isa. 45:9)—but we must be satisfied because of the wisdom and goodness of it. Whatever the bestowal of God's providence may be concerning those who wait on Him, we may be sure that even as He does them no wrong, He means them no hurt. No, they may say as the psalmist did, even when he was plagued all the day long and chastened every morning (Ps. 73:14), "However circumstances may be, yet *'God is good'* (v. 1)." *"Though he slay me, yet will I trust in him"* (Job 13:15), yet will I wait on Him.

I will expound on this duty of waiting on God by other Scriptures that speak the same thing. Like our text, these verses contain a great part of that homage that we are bound to pay to Him and that communion that it is our interest to keep up with Him. *"Truly our fellowship is with the Father, and with his Son Jesus Christ"* (1 John 1:3).

"I have set the LORD always before me" (Ps. 16:8). To wait on God is to set Him always before us. It is to look on Him as one always near us, always at our right hand, who has His eye upon us, wherever we are and whatever we are doing. It is to further see Him as one to whom we are accountable, *"with whom we have to do"* (Heb. 4:13), and in whom *"we live, and move, and have our being"* (Acts 17:28). This is pressed upon us as the great principle of gospel obedience: "Walk before me, and be upright." Walking at all times as before God and studying to approve ourselves to Him—herein consists the uprightness that is our evangelical perfection.

Experiencing God's Presence

"Mine eyes are ever toward the Lᴏʀᴅ" (Ps. 25:15). To wait on God is to have our eyes ever toward the Lord. Though we cannot see Him by reason of our present distance and darkness, we must look toward Him, toward the place where His honor dwells. We must look to Him as those who desire the knowledge of Him and His will. We must direct all to His honor as the mark we aim at, laboring that, *"whether present or absent, we may be accepted of him"* (2 Cor. 5:9). To wait on Him is to follow Him with our eyes in all those things wherein He is pleased to manifest Himself and to welcome the discoveries of His being and perfections.

"In all thy ways acknowledge him" (Prov. 3:6). To wait on God is to acknowledge Him in all our ways. In all the actions and affairs of life, we must walk in His hand and set ourselves in the way of His steps. In all our undertakings, we must wait on Him for direction and success and, by faith and prayer, commit our way to Him to undertake for us. We must take Him with us wherever we go. *"If thy presence go not with* [us], *carry us not up hence"* (Exod. 33:15). In all our comforts we must see His hand giving them out to us, and in all our crosses we must see the same hand laying them upon us, that we may learn to receive both good and evil and to bless the name of the Lord both when He gives and when He takes.

"Caleb...hath followed me fully" (Num. 14:24). To wait on the Lord is to follow Him fully, as Caleb

74

did. It is to *"have respect unto all* [His] *commandments"* (Ps. 119:6) and to study to *"stand...complete in all the will of God"* (Col. 4:12). Wherever God leads us and goes before us, we must be followers of Him as dear children; we must *"follow the Lamb whithersoever he goeth"* (Rev. 14:4) and take Him for our guide wherever we go.

This is what it means to wait on God. Those who wait on God may cheerfully wait for Him, for He will, without fail, appear in due time to their joy. That word of Solomon will be made good to them: *"He that waiteth on his master shall be honoured"* (Prov. 27:18), for Christ has said, *"Where I am, there shall also my servant be"* (John 12:26).

Chapter 5

Every Day, All Day

Our eyes wait upon the LORD our God.
—Psalm 123:2

H aving shown you what it means to wait on God, I will next show that we must do this every day and all the day long. It is the work of every day that is to be done in its day, for the duty of every day requires it. Servants in the courts of princes have their weeks or months of waiting appointed them and are obliged to attend only at certain times. But God's servants must never stop waiting; all the days of our appointed times, the time of our work and warfare here on the earth, we must be waiting. We must not desire or expect to be discharged from this attendance until we get to heaven, where we will wait on God, as angels do, more closely and constantly.

We must wait on God every day, on Sundays and on weekdays. The Lord's Day is instituted and appointed for our attendance upon God in the courts of His house. We must wait on Him there to give glory to Him and to receive both commands and favors from Him. Ministers must then wait on their ministry (Rom. 12:7), and the people must wait on it, too, saying as Cornelius said for himself and his friends, *"Now therefore are we all here present before God, to hear all things that are commanded thee of God"* (Acts 10:33). We honor God when we help fill up the assemblies of those who attend at the footstool of His throne. The entire time on Sundays, except what is taken up in works of necessity and mercy, must be employed in waiting on our God. Christians are spiritual priests, and as such it is their business to wait in God's house at the time appointed.

But that is not enough. We must wait on our God on weekdays, too, for every day of the week we need mercy from Him and have work to do for Him. Our waiting on Him in public ordinances on the first day of the week is designed to focus us on, and fit us for, communion with Him all the week after. Therefore, we do not carry out what was intended on Sunday unless its impressions abide on us, go with us into the business of the week, and are kept always in our hearts. Thus from one Sunday to another and from one new moon to another, we must stay holy and gracious. We must be in the Spirit on the Lord's Day to such an extent that we walk in the Spirit all the week.

On both idle days and busy days, we must be found waiting on God. Some days of our lives are days of labor and hurry, when our particular callings call for our diligence and determination, but we must not think that will excuse us from our constant attendance upon God. Even when our hands are working in the world, our hearts may be waiting on our God by a habitual regard to Him, to His providence as our guide, and to His glory as our goal in our worldly business. Thus we must abide with Him on busy days. Those who rise up early, sit up late, and eat the bread of anxieties (Ps. 127:2) in pursuit of the world, should still wait on God, because otherwise all their care and pains will signify nothing; it is labor in vain—no, it is labor in the fire.

On some days of our lives, we relax from business and take our ease. Many of you have your time for diversion, but when you lay aside other business, this time of waiting on God must not be laid aside. When you test yourself with mirth, as Solomon did, and say that you will enjoy pleasure a little (Eccl. 2:1), let this wisdom remain with you. Let your eye then look up to God, and do not drop your communion with Him while having what you call an agreeable conversation with your friends.

Whether it is a day of work or a day of rest, we will find nothing like waiting on God, both to lighten the toil of our work and to sweeten the comfort of our repose. So, whether we have much to do or little to do in the world, still we must wait on God so that we may be kept from the temptation that accompanies both the one and the other.

In days of prosperity and in days of adversity, we must be found waiting on God. Does the world smile upon us and please us? Yet let us not turn from attending upon God to try to please the world. If we have ever so much of the wealth of the world, we still cannot say we have no need of God. David was ready to say this. In his prosperity he said he would *"never be moved"* (Ps. 30:6). But he soon saw his error when God hid His face and he was troubled (v. 7).

When our affairs prosper and God gives plentifully into our hands, we must wait on God as our great landlord and acknowledge our obligations to Him. We must beg His blessing on what we have and His favor with it, and depend on Him for both the continuance and the comfort of it. We must wait on God for wisdom and grace to use what we have for the purposes for which He entrusted us with it. We must do so as those who must give account and do not know how soon. And no matter how much we have of this world and how richly it is given to us to enjoy, still we must wait on God for better things—not only better than the world gives, but better than He Himself gives in this world.

When the world frowns on us and things go very badly, we must not worry over its frowns or frighten ourselves with them so that we are driven off from waiting on God. Rather, let us thereby be driven to it. Afflictions are sent for this end, to bring us to the throne of grace, to teach us to pray, and to make the word of God's grace precious to us.

In the day of our sorrow, we must wait on God for those comforts that are sufficient to balance our griefs. Job, when in tears, fell down and worshiped God for taking away as well as giving. In the day of our fear, we must wait on God for those encouragements that are sufficient to silence our fears. Jehoshaphat in his distress waited on God, and it was not in vain: His heart was established by it. David, whose heart was also often strengthened, was brought to this resolution, which was an anchor to his soul: *"What time I am afraid, I will trust in thee"* (Ps. 56:3).

Both in the days of youth and in the days of old age, we must be found waiting on God. Those who are young cannot begin their attendance upon God too soon. The child Samuel ministered to the Lord, and the Scriptures put a particular mark of honor on his service. Also, Christ was wonderfully pleased with the hosannas of the children who waited on Him when He rode in triumph into Jerusalem. When Solomon in his youth ascended the throne and waited on God for wisdom, it is said, *"The speech pleased the Lord"* (1 Kings 3:10). *"I remember thee,"* says God to Israel, *"[even] the kindness of thy youth...when thou wentest after me* [and did wait on Me] *in the wilderness"* (Jer. 2:2).

To wait on God is to be mindful of our Creator, and the proper time for that is in the days of our youth. (See Ecclesiastes 12:1.) Those who would wait on God properly must learn to do it early; the most accomplished courtiers are those who are brought up at court.

And may the old servants of Jesus be dismissed from waiting on Him? No, their attendance is still required and will still be accepted. They will not be cast off by their Master in the time of old age, and therefore let them not desert His service. When, through the infirmities of age, they can no longer be working servants in God's family, they may be waiting servants.

Like King David's elderly friend Barzillai, there are those who are unfit for the entertainments of the courts of earthly princes. But they may relish the pleasures of God's courts as well as ever. The Levites, when they were past the age of fifty, were discharged from the toilsome part of their service, but they still had to wait on God—and so must we. We must be quietly waiting to give honor to Him and to receive comfort from Him.

Those who have done the will of God and completed their work have need of patience to enable them to wait until they inherit the promise (Heb. 10:36). The nearer the happiness is that they are waiting for, the dearer should be the God they are waiting on and hope shortly to be with, eternally.

We read that we must wait on our God all the day. Every day, from morning to night, we must continue waiting on God. Whatever change there may be in our employments, this must be the constant disposition of our souls. We must attend upon God and have our eyes ever toward Him. We must not at any time allow ourselves to wander from God or to attend upon anything besides Him, except, of course, what we attend upon for Him, in subordination to His will and in subserviency to His glory.

We must cast our daily cares on Him. Every day brings with it its fresh cares, more or less. These awake with us every morning, and we do not need to go so far as tomorrow to find problems: *"Sufficient unto the day is the evil thereof"* (Matt. 6:34). You who are great businesspeople in the world, you have your cares with you all the day. You may keep them to yourselves, yet they sit down with you and rise up with you; they go out and come in with you. They are more a load on you than those you converse with are aware of.

Some, through the weakness of their spirits, can scarcely determine anything except with fear and trembling.

Let this burden be cast on the Lord. Believe that His providence extends to all your affairs, to all events concerning you—even the most minute and seemingly accidental. Believe that your times are in His hand (Ps. 31:15) and all your ways at His disposal. Believe His promise, that all things will be made to work for good to those who love Him (Rom. 8:28). Then give to Him yourself and every circumstance to do with as seems good in His eyes. Rest satisfied in having done so, and resolve to be at peace.

Bring your cares to God by prayer in the morning, and spread them before Him. Then make it appear all through the day, by the composure and cheerfulness of your spirits, that you left your cares with Him as Hannah did. For, when she had prayed, she *"went her way, and did eat, and her countenance was no more sad"* (1 Sam. 1:18). Commit your way to the Lord, and then submit to His arranging of it, though it may go against your expectations. Bear yourself up upon the assurances God has given you, that He will care for you as the tender father for the child.

We must manage our daily business for Him, keeping in mind His providence, which has put us into the calling and employment that we are in.

We must all look to His precept, making diligence in it our duty. We must all look to His blessing, as that which is necessary to make our work comfortable and successful. And we must all look to His glory as our highest end in all. This sanctifies our common actions to God, sweetens them, and makes them pleasant to ourselves.

If Gaius brings his friends whom he is parting with a little way on their journey, it is only a small act of common civility. But if he does it in a godly way, if he pays respect to them because they belong to Christ and for Christ's sake, if he does it so that he may have more profitable communication with them, then it becomes an act of Christian piety. (See 3 John 1:6.) Here is a general rule by which we must govern ourselves in the business of every day: *"Whatsoever ye do in word or deed, do all in the name of the Lord Jesus"* (Col. 3:17). Thus, in and by the Mediator we wait on our God.

This rule is particularly recommended to servants, though their jobs are lowly and they are under the command of their masters. Nevertheless, let them do their servile works as the servants of Christ, *"as to the Lord, and not to men"* (Eph. 6:7). Let them work with singleness of heart as unto Christ, and they will be accepted by Him, and from Him they will receive the reward of the inheritance (Col. 3:22–24). Let them wait on God all the day when they are doing their day's work, by doing it faithfully and conscientiously, so that they may *"adorn the doctrine of God our Saviour"* (Titus 2:10) by aiming at His glory even in common business.

We work so that we may get bread; we get bread so that we may live; we live, not so that we may live for ourselves and please ourselves, but so that we may live for God and please Him. We work so that we may fill up time and fill up a place in the world, and because God, who has made and maintained us, has appointed for us to work with quietness and to mind our own business.

We must receive our daily comforts from Him. We must wait on Him as our benefactor. The eyes of all things wait on Him, to give them their food in due season; and what He gives them, that they gather (Ps. 104:27–28). Because He is our Father, we must look to Him for our daily bread. From Him we are appointed to ask it, yes, even if we have it in the house, even if we have it on the table. We must wait on Him for permission to make use of it, for a blessing on it, for nourishment by it, and for comfort in it. It is in the Word and prayer that we wait on God and keep up communion with Him. By these, every creature of God is sanctified to us, and the property of it is altered. *"Unto the pure all things are pure"* (Titus 1:15). They have their things from the covenant and not from common providence, making the little that the righteous man has better than the riches of many wicked (Ps. 37:16) and much more valuable and comfortable.

No inducement can be more powerful to get what we get honestly, and use it soberly, and give God His due out of it, than this consideration: We have our all from the hand of God and are entrusted with it as stewards and, consequently, are accountable. What we have is God's gifts; every bite we eat and every drop we drink is His mercy; every breath we breathe and every step we take, His mercy. If we have this thought as a golden thread running through all the comforts of every day, this will keep us continually waiting on Him, as the donkey on his master's trough, and will put a double sweetness into all our enjoyments.

God will have His mercies taken fresh from His compassions, which for this reason are said to be new every morning. Therefore, it is not once a week that we are to wait on Him, as people buy provisions for the whole week. But we must wait on Him every day and all the day, as those who live from hand to mouth and yet live very well.

We must resist our daily temptations and do our daily duties in the strength of His grace. Every day brings its temptation with it. Our Master knew this when He taught us to pray the following as consistently as we pray for our daily bread: *"Lead us not into temptation"* (Matt. 6:13). There is no business we engage in, no enjoyment we partake of, that does not have its snares accompanying it. Satan uses these things to assault us and to endeavor to draw us into sin.

Now sin is the great evil we should be continually on our guard against, as Nehemiah was. He recognized Satan's trap: *"That I should be afraid, and do so, and sin"* (Neh. 6:13). And we have no way to secure ourselves except by waiting on God all the day. We must not only put ourselves under the protection of His grace in the morning, but we must all the day keep ourselves under the shelter of it. We must not only go forth, but go forth in dependence on the grace that He has said will be sufficient for us and on the care that will not allow us to be tempted above what we are able (1 Cor. 10:13). Our waiting on God will furnish us with the best arguments to use in resisting temptations and with strength according to the day. *"Be strong in the Lord, and in the power of his might"* (Eph. 6:10), and then wait on the Lord all the day.

We have duties to do, and many opportunities to speak good words and do good works. And we must see and admit that we are not sufficient in ourselves for anything that is good, not so much as to think a good thought. We must therefore wait on God, must seek Him and depend on Him, for that light and fire, that wisdom and zeal, which are necessary to the due discharge of our duty. We must seek Him so that, by His grace, we may not only be fortified against every evil word and work, but also furnished for every good word and work. From the fullness that is in Jesus Christ, we must by faith be continually drawing grace upon grace—grace for all gracious exercises, grace to help in every time of need. We must wait on His grace, must follow the guidance of it, must comply with the operations of it, and must be turned to it as wax to the seal.

We must bear our daily afflictions with submission to His will. We are told to expect trouble in the flesh. Something or other happens every day that grieves us, something in our relations, something in our callings, events concerning ourselves, our families, or friends. Perhaps we have every day some bodily pain or sickness, or some cross and disappointment in our affairs. Now in these we must wait on God. Christ requires each of His disciples to take up his cross daily. We must not willfully pluck the cross down upon us, but we must take it up when God lays it in our way and not go a step out of the way of duty, either to meet it or to miss it. It is not enough to bear the cross, but we must take it up—we must accommodate ourselves to it and acquiesce to the will of God in it. Our attitudes must not be, "This is an evil, and I must bear it," but, "This is the will of God."

We must see every affliction as allotted to us by our heavenly Father, and in it we must discover His correcting hand. Therefore, we must wait on Him to know the reason why He contends with us, the fault for which He chastens us, the bad attitude that needs to be cured in us. Then we can fulfill God's purpose in afflicting us and so be made partakers of His holiness. We must watch the motions of Providence, we must keep our eyes upon our Father when He frowns, so that we may discover what His mind is and what the obedience is that we are to learn by the things that we suffer. (See Hebrews 5:8.)

We must wait on God for support under our burdens. We must put ourselves into the everlasting arms, which are laid under the children of God to sustain them when the rod of God is upon them. God is the one we must wait on for deliverance, not seeking to extricate ourselves by any sinful, indirect methods, nor looking to others for relief, but still waiting on the Lord until He has mercy on us (Ps. 123:2). We must be well content to bear the burden until God eases us of it, and eases us in mercy. If the affliction is lengthened, we must wait on the Lord, even when He hides His face, hoping that His wrath is little and for a small moment (Isa. 54:7–8).

We must anticipate the news and events of every day with a cheerful and entire resignation to the divine providence. While we are in this world, we are still expecting and hoping good and fearing ill. We do not know what a day, a night, or an hour will bring forth. And we are too apt to spend our thoughts in vain about future things, which happen quite differently from what we imagine. In all our prospects we must wait on God.

Are we hoping for good news, a good outcome? Let us wait on God as the giver of the good we hope for and be ready to take it from His hand and to meet Him with suitable affections when He is coming toward us with mercy. Whatever good we hope for, it is God alone, and His wisdom, power, and goodness, that we must hope in. Therefore, our hopes must be humble and modest and regulated by His will. What God has promised us, we may with assurance promise ourselves, and no more. If thus we wait on God in our hopes, if the hope is deferred, it will not make the heart sick. (See Proverbs 13:12.) For the God we wait on will overrule all for the best. But when the desire comes, in pursuit of which we have thus waited on God, we may see it coming from His love, and it will be a tree of life.

Are we in fear of bad news, of melancholy events, and of a sad outcome of affairs? Let us wait on God to be delivered from all our fears, from the things themselves we are afraid of, and from the awful, tormenting fears of them. When Jacob was with good reason afraid of his brother Esau, he waited on God, brought his fears to Him, wrestled with Him, and prevailed for deliverance! *"What time I am afraid,"* said David, *"I will trust in thee"* (Ps. 56:3). "I will wait on You," he said, "and that will establish the heart, so as to set it above the fear of evil tidings."

Are we in suspense between hope and fear? Sometimes one prevails and sometimes the other? Let us wait on God, as the God to whom belong the issues of life and death, good and evil, from whom our judgments, and every man's, proceed. And let us settle ourselves into a quiet expectation of the event, whatever it may be, with a resolution to accommodate ourselves to it. Hope for the best, and get ready for the worst, and then take what God sends.

Chapter 6

Opportunities for Waiting on God

A good man...will guide his
affairs with discretion.
—Psalm 112:5

L et me further urge upon you this duty of waiting on God all the day by giving you some more particular instances concerning what you have to do in the ordinary business of the day. We are weak and forgetful, and we need to be reminded of our general duty on every occasion that we have for doing it. Therefore, I will be very particular so that I may be your remembrancer.

When you meet with your family in the morning, wait on God for a blessing upon them, with thanksgiving for the mercies you and yours have jointly received from God the night past. You and your family must serve the Lord, must wait on Him. See it owing to His goodness, who is the Founder and Father of the families of the righteous, that you are together, that the voice of rejoicing and salvation is in your tabernacles (Ps. 118:15).

Therefore, wait on Him to keep you together, to make you a comfort to one another, to enable you to do your duty to every relation, and to lengthen the days of your tranquillity. In all the conversation we have with our families, the provision we make for them, and the orders we give concerning them, we must wait on God, as *"the God of all the families of Israel"* (Jer. 31:1). We must look to Christ, as He in whom all the families of the earth are blessed.

Every member of the family sharing in family mercies must wait on God for grace to contribute to family duties. Whatever disagreeableness there may be in any family relationship, instead of having the spirit either burdened with it or provoked by it, let it be an inducement to wait on God, who is able either to remedy the grievance or to balance it and give grace to bear it.

When you are pursuing the education of your children, wait on God for His grace to make the means of education successful. When you are yourself giving them instruction in things pertaining either to life or godliness, their general or particular calling, when you are sending them to school in the morning or giving them their duties for the day, wait on God to give them an understanding and a good capacity for their activities. It is God who gives wisdom. If they are slow and do not come along as you wish, wait on God to bring them forward and to give them His grace in His own time. While you are patiently waiting on Him, that will encourage you to take pains with them and will likewise make you patient and gentle toward them.

Let young people wait on God in all their daily endeavors, to fit themselves for the service of God and their generation. You desire to be a comfort to your family, to be good for something in this world, do you not? Then beg God for a wise and under-standing heart, as Solomon did. Wait on Him all the day for it, so that you may increase in wisdom, as you do in stature, and *"in favour with God and man"* (Luke 2:52).

When you go to your shop or apply yourself to the business of your particular calling, wait on God for His presence with you. Your business calls for your constant attendance every day and all the day. Keep the shop, and your shop will keep you. But let your attendance upon God in your calling be as constant as your attendance upon your call-ing. Study God's providence in daily occurrences.

Open your shop with this thought: I am now doing my duty, and I depend on God to bless me in it. When you are waiting for customers, wait on God to find you something to do in that calling to which He has called you. Those you refer to as chance customers, you should rather refer to as providence customers, and you should say of the profit you make by them, "The Lord my God brought it to me."

When you are buying and selling, see God's eye on you to observe whether you are honest and just in your dealings. Do no wrong to those you deal with. Look up to Him for the discretion that He teaches, the prudence that directs the way and with which it is promised the good man will order his affairs. Look to God for the blessing that makes rich and has no sorrow with it (Prov. 10:22), for the honest profit that may be expected by way of honest diligence.

Whatever your job may be, whether in a business or in the business of the home, go about it in the fear of God, depending on Him to make it comfortable and successful and to prosper the work of your hands. In this way, you will arm yourself against the many temptations you are surrounded with in your worldly business. By waiting on God, you will be freed from the care that comes with much serving, will have your mind raised above the little things of sense and time, will be serving God when you are most busy, and will have God in your heart when your hands are full of the world.

When you pick up a book—God's Book or any other useful, good book—wait on God for His grace to enable you to make good use of it. Some of you spend a good deal of time reading every day, and I hope none of you lets a day pass without reading some portions of Scripture, either alone or with your family. Be careful that the time you spend in reading is not lost time. It is lost if you read that which is idle and vain and unprofitable. It is lost if you read that which is good, even the Word of God itself, and do not obey it, observe it, or aim to make it of any advantage to you. Wait on God, who gives you those helps for your soul. The eunuch did so when he was reading the book of Isaiah in his chariot, and God sent him someone to help him understand what he read.

Perhaps you read a history book now and then. In acquainting yourself with history, you must have your eyes on God and on that wise and gracious Providence that governed the world before you were born and preserved the church. He may still be depended on to do all for the best. He is Israel's King of old.

When you sit down to your supper table, wait on God. See His hand preparing a table before you in spite of your enemies and in the society of your friends. Often review the grant that God made to our first father Adam, and in him to us, of the products of the earth. *"Behold, I have given you every herb bearing seed...to you it shall be for meat"* (Gen. 1:29). And review the grant he afterward made to Noah, our second father, and in him to us: *"Every moving thing that liveth shall be meat for you; even as the green herb"* (Gen. 9:3). See what a bountiful benefactor He is to mankind, and wait on Him accordingly.

We must eat and drink to the glory of God, and so we must wait on Him in eating and drinking. We must receive nourishment for our bodies so that they may be fitted to serve our souls in the service of God, for His honor in this world. We must taste covenant love in common mercies and enjoy the Creator while we are using the creature. We must depend on the word of blessing from the mouth of God to make our food nourishing to us. And if our provisions are scanty, we must make up the lack of them by faith in the promise of God. We must rejoice in Him, as the God of our salvation, though the fig tree does not blossom and there is no fruit on the vine (Hab. 3:17–18).

When you visit your friends, or receive their visits, wait on God. Look to Him with thankfulness for the comfort of your friends and acquaintances. Be thankful that you do not have to live in the wilderness or the solitary desert. Give thanks that you have comfort, not only in your own house, but also in those of your neighbors, with whom you have freedom of conversation. Be grateful that you are not driven out from among men and made a burden and terror to all those around you.

That you have clothing not only for necessity but also for ornament is a mercy. We must take notice of God in this so that we may not pride ourselves in it. *"I decked thee also with ornaments,"* says God, *"and I put...earrings in thine ears"* (Ezek. 16:11–12). That you have houses, furniture, and entertainment, not only for yourself, but also for your friends, is a mercy in which God must be acknowledged.

When we are among company, we must look up to God for wisdom to conduct ourselves so that we may do much good for, and get no harm by, those with whom we converse. Wait on God for that grace with which our speech should always be seasoned (Col. 4:6), and by which all corrupt communication may be prevented. Wait on God for grace to abound in that which is good, that which is edifying, and that which may minister grace to the hearers, so that your lips may feed many.

When you give alms or do any act of charity, wait on God. Do it as unto Him. Give to a disciple in the name of a disciple, to the poor because they belong to Christ. Do it not for the praise of men, but for the glory of God. With a single eye and an upright heart, direct it to Him. Then your alms as well as your prayers, like those of Cornelius, will *"come up for a memorial before God"* (Acts 10:4). Beg of God to accept what you do for the good of others, that your alms may indeed be offerings, that they may be *"an odour of a sweet smell, a sacrifice acceptable, wellpleasing to God"* (Phil. 4:18).

Desire from God a blessing upon what you give in charity, that it may give comfort to those to whom it is bestowed. Though what you are able to give is only a little, like the widow's two mites, yet that, by God's blessing, may be doubled and made to go a great way, like the widow's flour in the barrel and oil in the jar.

Depend on God to make up to you what you give out in good works and to recompense it abundantly in the resurrection of the just. No, you are encouraged to wait on Him for a return of it even in this life. It is bread cast upon the waters, which you will find again after many days (Eccl. 11:1). Carefully observe the providence of God. See if it will not richly compensate you for your good works, according to His promises, so that you may understand the loving-kindness of the Lord and His faithfulness to the word that He has spoken.

When you ask about the news, wait on God. Keep your eyes on Him. Do it for these reasons: because you are truly concerned for the interests of His kingdom in the world and lay them near your heart and because you have a compassion for mankind, for the lives and souls of men, and especially of God's people. Ask, "What's new?" not as the Athenians did, only to satisfy a vain curiosity and to pass away an idle hour or two. Find out the news so that you may know how to direct your prayers and praises, how to balance your hopes and fears, and so that you may gain such an understanding of the times that you will learn what you and others ought to do.

If the face of public affairs is bright and pleasing, wait on God to carry on and perfect His own work and do not depend on the wisdom or strength of any human instrument. If it is dark and discouraging, wait on God to prevent the fears of His people and to appear for them when He sees that their strength is gone. In the midst of the greatest successes of the church and the smiles of benevolent circumstances, we must not think it needless to wait on God. In the midst of the church's greatest discouragements, when its affairs are reduced to the last extremity, we must not think it fruitless to wait on God. His created beings cannot help without Him, but He can help without them.

When you are going on a journey, wait on God. Put yourself under His protection; commit yourself to His care. Depend on Him to give His angels a charge concerning you, to bear you up in their arms when you move, and to pitch their tents around you where you rest. See how much you are indebted to the goodness of His providence for all the comforts and conveniences you are surrounded with in your travels. It is He who has put us in a land where we do not wander in wildernesses, as in the deserts of Arabia, but have safe roads; the highways are not unoccupied because of the terrors of war. Because of Him, our going out and coming in are preserved. When we are abroad, we are not in banishment, but have liberty to come home again. When we are at home, we are not under confinement, but have liberty to go abroad.

We must therefore have our eyes up to God when we set out: "Lord, go along with me where I go." Under His shelter we must travel, confiding in His care of us and encouraging ourselves with that in all the dangers we meet. In our return trips, we must acknowledge His goodness. All our bones must say, *"Lord, who is like unto thee"* (Ps. 35:10), for He keeps all our bones—not one of them is broken (Ps. 34:20).

When we retire into solitude, to be alone on a walk, or alone resting in our bedrooms, still we must be waiting on God. Still we must keep up our communion with Him when we are communing with our own hearts. When we are alone, we must not be alone, but the Father must be with us, and we with Him. We will find temptations even in solitude. We need to guard against these temptations. Satan tempted our Savior when He was alone in a wilderness.

In solitude we also have the opportunity, if we know how to take it, for devout and divine contemplation. We have time for communion with God, which is the best conversation. We are never less alone than when we are alone with God.

Many moments we spend silently alone, withdrawn from business and conversation. If we have the art, I should say the *heart,* to fill up those vacant minutes with pious meditations of God and divine things, we then gather up the fragments of time, so that nothing may be lost. So we are found waiting on God all the day.

Let me give you some reasons why you must live a life of communion with God by waiting on Him all the day.

Consider that the eye of God is always upon you. When we are with our superiors, and we see them look at us, that prompts us to look at them. Should we not then look up to God, whose eyes always behold, and whose eyelids try, the children of men (Ps. 11:4)? He sees all the motions of our hearts and sees with pleasure the motions of our hearts toward Him. This should cause us to set Him always before us.

The servant, even if he is careless at other times, will wait in his place and pay close attention to his business when he is under his master's eye. We need no more to make us diligent than to do our work while our Master looks on. Then we are diligent because He is looking at us, and we will never be distracted.

The God you are to wait on is one with whom you have to do. *"All things,"* even the thoughts and intents of the heart, *"are naked and opened unto the eyes of him with whom we have to do"* (Heb. 4:13). *"Him with whom we have to do"* means one with whom we have business or words, who has something to say to us, and to whom we have something to say. Or, some say it means one to whom there is a reckoning, a running account between us and Him. Indeed, every one of us must soon give account of ourselves to God and of everything done in the body. Therefore, it is our concern to wait on Him that all may be made right daily between us and Him, in the blood of Christ, which balances the account. If we would consider how much we have to do with God every day, we would be more diligent and constant in our attendance upon Him.

The God we are to wait on continually waits to be gracious to us. He is always doing us good, preceding us with the blessings of His goodness, and daily loading us with His benefits (Ps. 68:19).

He loses no opportunity of showing His care for us when we are in danger, His bounty to us when we are in need, and His tenderness for us when we are in sorrow. His good providence waits on us all the day, to preserve our going out and our coming in, to give us relief and help in due season. Indeed, His good grace waits on us all the day to help us in every time of need, to be strength to us according to our days, and all the occurrences of the days. When God is this forward to do us good, should we be backward and remiss in doing Him service?

If we attend upon God, His holy angels will have a charge to attend upon us. They are all appointed to be *"ministering spirits,"* to minister for the good of those *"who shall be heirs of salvation"* (Heb. 1:14). They do more good things for us every day than we are aware of. What an honor, what a privilege it is, to be waited on by holy angels, to be borne up in their arms, to be surrounded by their tents! What a security is the ministration of those good spirits against the malice of evil spirits! This honor belongs to all who wait on God all the day.

This life of communion with God and constant attendance upon Him is a heaven on earth. It is doing the work of heaven and the will of God as the angels who are in heaven do it, whose business it is to always behold the face of our Father (Matt. 18:10). It is a pledge of the blessedness of heaven; it is a preparation for it, and a prelude to it. It is having our citizenship in heaven, from which we look for the Savior (Phil. 3:20). Looking for Him as our Savior, we look to Him as our Director. By this we make it to appear that our hearts are there, which will give us good ground to expect that we will be there shortly.

Let me close this chapter with some directions of what you must do so that you may wait on God all the day.

See much of God in every creature—of His wisdom and power in making and placing it, and of His goodness in its usefulness to us. Look around you, and see what a variety of wonders, what an abundance of comforts, you are surrounded with. Let them all lead you to Him who is the Fountain of being and the Giver of all good. All our springs are in Him, and from Him are all our streams. This truth will cause us to wait on Him, since every creature is to us what He makes it to be. Thus the same things that draw a carnal heart from God will lead a gracious soul to Him. And, since all His works praise Him, His saints will take continual occasion to bless Him.

The custom of the pious Jews of old, so they say, was to give God the glory for whatever delight they took in any creature. When they smelled a flower, they said, "Blessed be He who made this flower sweet." If they ate a morsel of bread,

"Blessed be He who appointed bread to strengthen man's heart." In the same way, if we taste in everything that the Lord is gracious, if we derive all satisfaction from His bounty, we will be zealous to constantly depend on Him, as the child depends on the mother's breast.

See every creature to be nothing without God. The more we discern the vanity and emptiness of the world and its utter insufficiency to make us happy, the closer we will cling to God, and the more intimately we will converse with Him. Then we will find the satisfaction in the Father of spirits that we sought for in vain in material things.

What folly it is to pursue mere creatures and to dance at their door, from which we are sure to be sent away empty. We have the Creator Himself to go to, who is rich in mercy to all who call on Him, who is full and free and faithful! What can we expect from lying vanities? Why then should we observe them and neglect our own mercies? Why should we trust in broken reeds, when we have a Rock of Ages to be the foundation of our hopes? And why should we draw from broken cisterns, when we have the God of all consolation to be the fountain of our joys?

Live by faith in the Lord Jesus Christ. We cannot with any confidence wait on God, except in and through a Mediator, for it is by His Son that God speaks to us and hears from us. All that passes between a just God and poor sinners must pass through the hands of that blessed Man, who has laid His hand upon them both. Every prayer passes from us to God, and every mercy from God to us, by that hand.

It is in the face of the Anointed that God looks upon us and in the face of Jesus Christ that we behold the glory and grace of God shining. It is by Christ that we have access to God and success with Him in prayer. Therefore, we must make mention of His righteousness and His alone. We must live upon God all day long in this manner. We must constantly depend on Him who always appears in the presence of God for us, who is always ready to introduce us.

Be frequent and serious in short, exclamatory prayers. In waiting on God, we must often speak to Him, must take all occasions to speak to Him. When we do not have an opportunity for a solemn address to Him, He will accept a sudden address, if it comes from an honest heart. In this way David waited on God all day, as we see in Psalm 25:1: *"Unto thee, O Lord, do I lift up my soul."* To You do I send it and all its gracious breathings after You.

We should in holy exclamations ask pardon for this sin, strength against that corruption, victory over this temptation. Our asking will not be in vain. This is what it means to pray always and without ceasing. It is not the length or language of the prayer that God looks at but the sincerity of the heart in it. Our sincere prayer will be accepted, even if the prayer is very short and the groanings are such that they cannot be uttered.

Look at every day as if it may be your last day. *"In such an hour as ye think not the Son of man cometh"* (Matt. 24:44). Therefore, we cannot on any morning be sure that we will live until night. We hear of many who have died very suddenly. What sort of people therefore ought we to be in all holy conduct and godliness (2 Pet. 3:11)? Though we cannot say that this day will be our last, we ought to live as if we were sure it would be. We know the Day of the Lord will come; therefore, we must wait on Him. For on whom should poor, dying creatures wait, but on a living God?

Death will bring us all to God, to be judged by Him; it will bring all the saints to Him, to the vision and enjoyment of Him. The One we are hastening to and hope to be forever with, we will want to wait on and cultivate an acquaintance with. If we thought more about death, we would converse more with God. Our dying daily is a good reason for our worshiping daily. Therefore, wherever we are, we should keep near to God because we do not know where death will meet us. Doing so will alter the property of death. Enoch, who walked with God, *"was translated that he should not see death"* (Heb. 11:5). Walking with God will furnish us with what we need on the other side of death and the grave.

If we continue waiting on God every day and all the day long, we will grow more experienced and consequently more expert in the great mystery of communion with God. Thus our last days will become our best days, our last works our best works, and our last comforts our sweetest comforts. In consideration of this, take the prophet's advice: *"Turn thou to thy God: keep mercy and judgment, and wait on thy God continually"* (Hos. 12:6).

Chapter 7

Rest after the Day's End

I will both lay me down in peace, and sleep:
for thou, LORD, only makest me
dwell in safety.
—Psalm 4:8

This verse may be understood figuratively: The soul rests in the assurance of God's grace. Or it may be taken literally: The body rests under the protection of His providence. I love to give Scripture its full range, and therefore, I embrace both interpretations.

Spiritual Rest

The psalmist, having chosen God's favor above any good, here expresses his great satisfaction in the choice he had made. He had seen many people making themselves perpetually uneasy with that fruitless inquiry, *"Who will show us any good?"* (Ps. 4:6), wearying themselves for their very vanity. But he had made himself perfectly peaceful by casting himself upon the divine good-will: *"LORD, lift thou up the light of thy countenance upon us"* (v. 6).

Any good thing short of God's favor will not satisfy us. But God's favor is enough, without the world's smiles. The moon, the stars, and all the candles in the world will not make day without the sun, but the sun will make day without any of them. These were David's sentiments, and all the saints agree with him. Finding no rest there-fore like Noah's dove in a deluged, defiled world, he flies to the ark of safety, which is Christ. *"Return unto thy rest* [unto your "Noah," which is the word in the original, for Noah's name signifies rest], *O my soul"* (Ps. 116:7).

If God lifts up the light of His countenance upon us, it fills us with a holy joy, and it puts more gladness into our hearts than that of those whose corn and wine increase (Ps. 4:7). We are then fixed in a holy rest. I will lay me down and sleep. God is my God, and I am pleased. I am satisfied, I look no further, I desire no more, I dwell in safety and confidence. While I walk in the light of the Lord, I neither lack any good nor am sensible of any deficiency, so I neither fear any evil nor am apprehensive of any danger. The Lord God is to me both *"a sun and shield"* (Ps. 84:11)—a sun to enlighten and comfort me, a shield to protect and defend me.

There is a lesson in all this: Those who have the assurances of God's favor toward them may enjoy, and should labor after, a holy serenity and security of mind. We have both of these put together in that precious promise, *"The work of righteousness shall be peace"* (Isa. 32:17). There is a present satisfaction in doing good; and in the final outcome, the effect of righteousness will be quietness and assurance forever—quietness in the enjoyment of good and assurance in a freedom from evil.

A holy serenity is one blessed fruit of God's favor: *"I will both lay me down in peace, and sleep."* While we are under God's displeasure or in doubt concerning His favor, how can we have any enjoyment of ourselves? While this great concern is unsettled, the soul cannot be satisfied. Does God have a controversy with you? *"Give not sleep to thine eyes, nor slumber to thine eyelids"* (Prov. 6:4) until you have taken care of the controversy. *"Go, humble thyself, and make sure thy friend"* (Prov. 6:3), for God is your Best Friend.

When you have made your peace with Him and have some comforting evidence that you are accepted by Him, then say wisely and justly what that carnal worldling said foolishly and without ground: *"Soul...take thine ease"* (Luke 12:19). For

113

in God, and in the covenant of grace, you have goods laid up for many years, goods laid up for eternity. Are your sins pardoned? Do you have an interest in Christ's mediation? Does God now in Him accept your works? *"Go thy way, eat thy bread with joy, and drink thy wine with a merry heart"* (Eccl. 9:7). Let His acceptance still every storm; let it command and create a calm in your soul.

When we have God to be our God in covenant, we have enough, we have all. Though the gracious soul still desires more of God, it never desires more than God. In Him it reposes itself with a perfect satisfaction. In Him it is at home, it is at rest. If we are such that we are satisfied only by His loving-kindness, we will indeed be satisfied with His loving-kindness, abundantly satisfied. There is enough in this to satiate the weary soul, to replenish every sorrowful soul (Jer. 31:25), to fill even the hungry with good things, with the best things. Being filled, they should be at rest, at rest forever, and their sleep here should be sweet.

A holy security is another blessed fruit of God's favor. *"Thou, Lord, only makest me dwell in safety."* When the light of Your countenance shines upon me, I am safe. I know I am safe, and therefore I am at peace. With Your favor You will compass me as with a shield (Ps. 5:12). Being taken under the protection of the divine favor, even if a host of enemies encamps against me, my heart will not fear; in spite of this I will be confident (Ps. 27:3). Whatever God has promised me, I can promise myself, and that is enough to secure me and save me unharmed, whatever difficulties and dangers I may meet with in the way of my duty.

Though the earth be removed, we will not fear (Ps. 46:2). We will fear no evil, no, not in the valley of the shadow of death, in the territories of the King of Terrors himself. For there You are with me; Your rod and Your staff comfort me (Ps. 23:4). What the rich man's wealth is to him, in his own imagination—a strong city and a high wall (Prov. 18:11)—that is what the good man's God is to him. The Almighty will be your gold, your defense.

Nothing is more dangerous than security in a sinful path. How dangerous when men cry, "Peace, peace," to themselves while they continue under the reigning power of a vain and carnal mind! Oh, that the sinners who are at ease were made to tremble! Nothing is more foolish than a security built on the world and its promises, for they are all vanity and a lie.

But nothing is more reasonable in itself, or more advantageous to us, than for good people to build assurances upon the promises of a good God. Nothing is more reasonable than for those who walk in the way of duty to be free from the fear of evil, for them to know that no evil will befall them, no real evil, no evil except what will be made to work for their good. Nothing is more reasonable than for those who continue in their allegiance to God as their king to know that they are under His protection. They are under the protection of omnipotence itself, which enables them to bid defiance to all malignant powers. *"If God be for us, who can be against us?"* (Rom. 8:31).

Even the heathen consider every honest, virtuous man to be entitled to this security, saying, "He whose life is upright and free from iniquity, if the world would fall in pieces about him, need not fear being lost in the desolations of it." Christians, who hold fast their integrity, have much more reason to lay claim to this serenity, for who or what can harm us if we are followers of Him who is exceedingly good?

It is the privilege of good people that they may be tranquil and satisfied. This holy serenity and security of mind is allowed them. God gives them permission to be cheerful; and what is more, God promises that He will speak peace to His people and to His saints. He will fill them *"with all joy and peace in believing"* (Rom. 15:13). His peace will keep their hearts and minds—keep them safe, keep them calm.

There is a method appointed for their obtaining this promised serenity and security. The Scriptures are written to them that their joy may be full, and that through patience and comfort of them they may have hope. Ordinances are instituted to be wells of salvation, out of which they may draw water with joy. Ministers are ordained to be their comforters and the helpers of their joy. Thus, God has been *"willing…to show unto the heirs of promise the immutability of his counsel* [so that they] *might have a strong consolation"* (Heb. 6:17–18).

It is the duty of good people to labor after this holy security and serenity of mind and to use the means appointed for obtaining it. Do not give way to the disquieting suggestions of Satan and to those tormenting doubts and fears that arise in your own soul. *"Study to be quiet"* (1 Thess. 4:11). Chide yourself for your distrusts. Charge yourself to believe and to hope in God, for you will yet praise Him.

If you are in the dark concerning yourself, do as Paul's mariners did: Cast anchor and wish for the day. Poor, trembling Christian, tossed with tempest and not comforted, try to lie down in peace and sleep. Compose yourself into a sedate and even frame of mind. In the name of Him whom winds and seas obey, command your tumultuous thoughts, and say, *"Peace, be still"* (Mark 4:39). Lay that aching, trembling head of yours where the beloved disciple laid his, in the bosom of the Lord Jesus. Or, if you have not yet attained such boldness of access to Him, lay that aching, trembling heart of yours at the feet of the Lord Jesus by an entire submission and resignation to Him. Say, "If I perish, I will perish here."

Put the matter into His hand by an entire confidence in Him. Submit it to His operation and disposal, for He knows how to speak to the heart. And if you have not yet entered into this present rest that remains for the people of God (Heb. 4:9), look at it as a land of promise. Though it tarries, wait for it, for the vision is for an appointed time; at the end it will speak and will not lie (Hab. 2:3). Light is sown for the righteous, and what is sown will come up again at last in a harvest of joy.

Physical Rest

Picture the scene in Psalm 4: The psalmist had done his day's work and had perhaps fatigued himself with it. It was bedtime, and he gave good advice to those to whom he wished a good night; he advised them to commune with their own hearts upon their beds and to offer the evening sacrifices of righteousness (vv. 4–5). He retired to his chamber with this word: *"I will both lay me down in peace, and sleep"* (v. 8). I am led to take this verse literally; it is speaking of taking rest in sleep.

And so we have here David's pious thoughts when he was going to bed. Just as David was still with God when he awoke, so he was still with God when he went to sleep. He concluded the day as he opened it, with meditations on God and sweet communion with Him.

It seems that David penned Psalm 4 when he was distressed and persecuted by his enemies. Perhaps it was penned on the same occasion as the foregoing psalm, when he fled from Absalom his son. *"Without were fightings,"* and no wonder that *"within were fears"* (2 Cor. 7:5). Yet then he put such a confidence in God's protection that he would go to bed at his usual time and, with his usual quietness and cheerfulness, would compose himself as at other times.

He knew that his enemies have no power against him except what was given them from above (John 19:11), and they would have no power given them except what was still under the divine check and restraint. Nor would their power be permitted to exert itself so far as to do him any real harm. Therefore, he retired into the secret place of the Most High, abode under the shadow of the Almighty (Ps. 91:1), and was very quiet in his own mind. What will break a worldly man's heart will not break a godly man's sleep. "Let them do their worst," said David. "I will lay me down and sleep; the will of the Lord be done."

Now observe here his confidence in God: *"Thou, Lord, only makest me dwell in safety."* You not only make me safe, but You also make me know that I am so. You cause me to dwell with a good assurance. It is the same idea used in Proverbs 10:9: *"He that walketh uprightly walketh surely."* In other words, he went boldly in his way. So David here went boldly to his bed. He did not dwell carelessly like the men of Laish (see Judges 18:7), but he dwelt at ease in God, like the sons of Zion in the city of their sacred feasts, when their eyes see it is a quiet habitation. (See Isaiah 33:20.)

There is a word in this part of the text that is notable; it is the word *only*. *"Thou, LORD, only makest me dwell in safety."* Some say this refers to David, who could say, "Even when I am alone, with none of my counselors around me to advise me, with none of my guards to fight for me, I am under no apprehension of danger while God is with me." Others say the meaning of Psalm 4:8 is that God is our protector. *"Thou, LORD, only makest me dwell in safety"*; it is done by You alone. Let us look at these two meanings separately.

Certainly the verse could apply to David. It could also apply to the Son of David, who comforted Himself with this fact—that when all His disciples forsook Him and left Him alone, He was not alone, for the Father was with Him.

Some weak people are afraid of being alone, especially in the dark. But a firm belief that God's presence is with us in all places and a belief that all good people are under His divine protection would silence those fears and make us ashamed of them.

Furthermore, our specialness as God's people, whom He has set apart for Himself, will be our security. Our singularity will be our safety and satisfaction, as Noah's was in the old world. Israel is a people who will dwell alone and will not be reckoned among the nations. Therefore, they may set all the nations at defiance until they foolishly mingle themselves among them. *"Israel then shall dwell in safety alone"* (Deut. 33:28). The more we dwell alone, the more safely we dwell.

But, as I said, the other meaning of Psalm 4:8 is that God is our protector, and this, I think, is the primary meaning of the verse. God does not need any assistance in protecting His people, though He sometimes makes use of instruments. *"The earth helped the woman"* (Rev. 12:16), yet He can do it without earthly instruments. When all our refuges fail, His own arm works salvation: *"So the Lord alone did lead him, and there was no strange god with him"* (Deut. 32:12). Yet that is not all. I depend on You alone to do it; therefore I am calm and consider myself safe, not because I have hosts on my side but solely because I have the Lord of Hosts on my side.

You make me to dwell in safety. This statement looks either backward or forward, or, rather, both. David was saying, "You have made me to dwell in safety all day so that the sun has not smitten me by day." It is the language of his thankfulness for the mercies he had received. David was also saying, "You will make me to dwell in safety all night, so that the moon will not smite me by night." (See Psalm 121:6.) It is the language of his dependence on God for further mercies. Thankfulness for past mercies and dependence for future mercies should go together. Our eyes must look to God as always the same, who *"was, and is, and is to come"* (Rev. 4:8), who has delivered, and does, and will.

Observe David's composure in Psalm 4:8. *"I will both lay me down in peace, and sleep."* They who have their corn and wine increasing, who have an abundance of the wealth and pleasure of this world, lie down and sleep contentedly, like Boaz at the end of the heap of corn (Ruth 3:7). But though I do not have what they have, I can lie down in peace and sleep as well as they.

We join them together, his lying down and his sleeping. I will not only lay me down as one who desires to be tranquil, but will also sleep as one who really is so. Some make the text to hint his falling asleep soon after he had lain down, so well wearied was he with the work of the day and so free from any of those disquieting thoughts that would keep him from sleeping.

In Psalm 4:8 are words with which to compose ourselves when we go to bed at night. We should take care to manage ourselves all day, especially when it draws toward night, so that we may not be unfit and out of condition for our evening devotions. We must take care that our hearts are not weighed down, either on the one hand with gluttony and drunkenness, as is often the case with men of pleasure; or, on the other hand, with the cares of this life, as is often the case with men of business. We should have such a command, both of our thoughts and of our time, that we may finish our daily work well, which will be a token of our finishing our lives' work well. And all is well indeed that ends everlastingly well.

Chapter 8

Closing the Day with God

I will both lay me down in peace, and sleep:
for thou, LORD, only makest me
dwell in safety.
—Psalm 4:8

As we must begin each morning with God and wait on Him all the day, so we must endeavor to close it with Him. I do not know how to better explain this duty of closing the day with God than by going over the same text and recommending to you David's example.

Hindrances to a Decent Bedtime

Nature calls for rest as well as food. Man goes forth to his work and labor. He goes to and fro about his duty. But it is only until evening, and then it is time to lie down. We read of Ishbosheth, that he lay on his bed at noon, but death met him there (2 Sam. 4:5–7). We read of David himself, that he arose from his bed one evening, but sin, a thing worse than death, met him there (2 Sam. 11:2–4).

We must work the works of Him who sent us while it is day. There will be time enough to lie down when the night comes and no man can work. It is then proper and seasonable to lie down. It is promised, *"They* [will] *lie down in the evening"* (Zeph. 2:7), and with that promise we must comply and rest in the time appointed for rest. We should not turn day into night, and night into day, as many do for some sinful reason or other.

Some, for example, sit up to do mischief to their neighbors, to kill, and steal, and to destroy. *"In the dark they dig through houses, which they had marked for themselves in the daytime"* (Job 24:16). David complained of his enemies, that at evening they *"go round about the city"* (Ps. 59:6). Say then, while others sit up watching for an opportunity to be mischievous, "I will lie down and be quiet and do no one any harm."

Those who do evil hate the light. Judas the traitor was in quest of his Master, with his band of men, when he should have been in bed. It shows an increase in the wickedness of the wicked when they take so many pains to devise a wicked plan and have their hearts so much upon it that they do not sleep unless they have done mischief (Prov. 4:16). It is a shame to those who profess to make it their business to do good that they cannot find in their hearts to give up any of their physical gratifications in pursuance of good.

Others sit up in the pursuit of the world and the wealth of it. They do not rise up early, but they sit up late in the eager pursuit of their covetous practices. Either to get or save, they deny themselves their most necessary sleep. This is their folly, for hereby they deprive themselves of the comfortable enjoyment of what they have—which is the end—under pretense of care and pains to obtain more—which is only the means.

Solomon speaks of the man who *"neither day nor night seeth sleep with his eyes"* (Eccl. 8:16), who makes himself a perfect slave to the world, and there is not a more cruel taskmaster than the world. Thus he makes that which is already vanity to be vexation of spirit. Men of this sort *"weary themselves for very vanity"* (Hab. 2:13). They are so miserably in love with their chains that they deny themselves, not only the spiritual rest God has provided for them as the God of grace, but also the natural rest, which, as the God of nature, He has provided.

This is an example of the wrong sinners do to their own bodies as well as their own souls. Let us see the folly of it and never labor thus for the meat that perishes and the abundance of the rich that will not allow them to sleep. Let us labor for the meat that endures to eternal life, the grace that is the pledge of glory, and the abundance of which will make our sleep sweet to us.

Others sit up in the indulgence of their pleasures. They will not lie down at a decent time because they cannot find in their hearts to leave their vain sports and pastimes, their music, dancing, plays, cards, and dice. Or, what is worse, they will not leave their rioting and excess, for they that are drunk, are drunk in the night (1 Thess. 5:7). It is bad enough when these gratifications of an evil lust, or at least of a vain mind, are allowed to devour the whole evening. They engross the whole soul, as they are apt enough to do insensibly, so that there is neither time nor heart for the evening devotions, either in private or with the family. But it is much worse when they are allowed to go far into the night, too; for then, of course, they trespass upon the ensuing morning and steal away the time that should then also be bestowed upon the exercise of religion.

Those who, with so much pleasure, sit up until I know not what time of night to make, as they say, "a merry night of it," to spend their time in filthiness and foolish talking and jesting would think themselves harshly dealt with if they should be kept one half hour past their sleeping time engaged in any good duties. They would have called Paul himself a tedious preacher and would have censured him as very indiscreet when, on a particular occasion, he continued his preaching until midnight. And how reluctant they would be to rise up at midnight, as David did, and give thanks to God, or to continue all night in prayer, as Jesus did.

Let the corrupt inclinations that cause us to transgress be mortified and not gratified. Those who have allowed themselves to indulge in such behaviors, if they have allowed themselves an impartial reflection, have doubtless found the harm in them. These indulgences have been a hindrance to the prosperity of the soul and should therefore be denied for our own good. One rule for the proper closing of the day is to keep good hours. Everything is beautiful in its season. I heard it said long ago, and I beg permission to repeat it now, that

> Early to bed, and early to rise,
> Is the way to be healthy, and wealthy, and wise.

I will now take it for granted that unless some necessary business or some work of mercy or some out-of-the-ordinary act of devotion keeps you up beyond your usual time, you will lay yourself down. And let us lie down with thankfulness to God, with thoughts of dying, with penitent reflections upon the sins of the day, and with humble supplications for the mercies of the night.

Causes for Gratitude

Let us lie down with thankfulness to God. When we retire to our bedrooms or prayer closets, we should lift up our hearts to God, the God of our mercies, and make Him the God of our praises. Whenever we go to bed, I am sure we do not lack matter for praise if we do not lack a heart. Let us therefore address ourselves to that pleasant duty, the work that is its own wages. The evening sacrifice was to be a sacrifice of praise.

We have reason to be thankful for the many mercies of the day past. We ought to carefully review them and say, *"Blessed be the Lord, who daily loadeth us with benefits"* (Ps. 68:19). Observe the constant series of mercies, which has not been interrupted on any single day. Observe the particular instances of mercy, which have made certain days stand out as remarkable. It is He who has granted us life and favor. It is His visitation that preserves our spirits.

Think how many calamities we are preserved from each and every day. Think about the calamities that we have been exposed to and delivered from, as well as those that we have not even been aware of, many of which we have deserved and which have befallen others better than we are. All our bones have reason to say, *"LORD, who is like unto thee?"* (Ps. 35:10). For it is God who keeps all our bones; *"not one of them is broken"* (Ps. 34:20).

Closing the Day with God

"It is of the LORD's mercies that we are not consumed" (Lam. 3:22).

Think how many comforts we are surrounded with every day, all of which make us indebted to the bounty of the divine providence. Every bit we eat, every drop we drink, is mercy. Every step we take, every breath we breathe, mercy. All the satisfaction we have in the affections of our relationships and in the society of our friends; all the success we have in our callings and jobs and the pleasure we take in them—these are what we have reason to acknowledge with thankfulness to God.

Yet it is likely that the day has not passed without some unfortunate accident. If something or other has afflicted and disappointed us, that must not indispose us to praise. However things may be, yet God is good; and it is our duty in everything to give thanks and to bless the name of the Lord, when He takes away as well as when He gives. For our afflictions are but few, and a thousand times deserved; our mercies are many, and a thousand times undeserved.

We have reason to be thankful for the shadows of the evening, which call us to retire and lie down. The same wisdom, power, and goodness that make the morning, make the evening also to rejoice. God gives us cause to be thankful for the drawing of the curtains of the night in favor of our repose, as well as for the opening of the eyelids in the morning in favor of our business.

When God divided between the light and the darkness and allotted to both of them their time successively, He saw that it was good. In a world of mixtures and changes, nothing was more proper. Let us therefore give thanks to the God who forms the light and creates the darkness. Believe, also, that the darkness of affliction may be as necessary for us in its season as the light of prosperity. If the hired worker longs until the shadow comes, let him be thankful for it when it does come that the burden and heat of the day are not perpetual.

We have reason to be thankful for a quiet place to lie down in, that we are not driven out from among men as Nebuchadnezzar to lie down with the beasts of the field. We do not have the wilderness for our habitation and the desolate and barren land for our dwelling. We are not forced to wander in deserts and mountains, in dens and caves of the earth, as many of God's dear saints and servants have been forced to do, *"of whom the world was not worthy"* (Heb. 11:38). But the Good Shepherd makes us to lie down in green pastures. We can be thankful that we do not have, as Jacob had, the cold ground for our bed and a stone for our pillow—which, however, one would be content with and covet if with it he could have Jacob's dream.

We have reason to be thankful that we are not forced to sit up, that our Master not only allows us to lie down but also orders that nothing should prevent our lying down. Many go to bed but cannot lie down there because of painful sicknesses of the nature that if they lie down they cannot breathe. Our bodies are of the same mold, and it is of the Lord's mercies that we are not similarly afflicted.

Many are kept up by sickness in their families. Children are ill, and they must attend them. If God takes sickness away from the midst of us and keeps it away so that no plague comes near our dwellings—if we have a large family and all are well—it is a mercy we are bound to be very thankful for. We should value it in proportion to the greatness of the affliction where sickness prevails.

Many are kept up by the fear of enemies, soldiers, or thieves. The head of the house watches so that his house may not be broken into. But our lying down is not prevented or disturbed by the alarms of war. We are delivered from the noise of battle in the places of our repose. There, consequently, we should retell the righteous acts of the Lord, even His righteous acts toward the inhabitants of His villages, which, under His protection, are as safe as walled cities with gates and bars. When we lie down, let us thank God that we may lie down.

Thoughts of Death

Let us lie down with thoughts of death and of the great change that at death we must pass under. The conclusion of every day should put us in mind of the conclusion of all our days when our night will come, our long night, which will put an end to our work and bring those of us who are honest laborers to our rest and wages.

It is good for us to think frequently of dying, to think of it as often as we go to bed. It will help to mortify the corruptions of our own hearts, which are our daily burdens. It will help to arm us against the temptations of the world, which are our daily snares. It will wean us from our daily comforts and comfort us under our daily crosses and fatigues. It is good for us to think familiarly of dying, to think of it as our going to bed. Thinking about it often and thinking about it in this way helps us get above the fear of it.

At death, we will retire as we do at bedtime; we will go to be private for a while, until the public appearance at the Great Day. *"Man lieth down, and riseth not: till the heavens be no more."* Until then, *"they shall not awake, nor be raised out of their sleep"* (Job 14:12). Now we go abroad to see and be seen, and to no higher purpose do some spend their days and spend their lives. But when death comes, there is an end of both. We will then see no more in this world; *"I shall behold man no* more" (Isa. 38:11). We will then be seen no more; *"the eye of him that hath seen me shall see me no more"* (Job 7:8). We will be hid in the grave and cut off from all living. To die is to bid "good night" to all our friends, to end our conversations with them. We bid them farewell, but, blessed be God, it is not an eternal farewell. We hope to meet them again in the morning of the Resurrection, to part no more.

At death, we will put off the body, as we put off our clothes when we lie down. The soul is the man; the body is only the clothes. At death, we will be unclothed. The earthly house of this tabernacle will be dissolved; the garment of the body will be laid aside. Death strips us and sends us naked out of the world as we came into it. It strips the soul of all the disguises wherein it appeared before men that it may appear naked and open before God. Our grave clothes are nightclothes.

When we are weary and hot, our clothes are a burden. We are very willing to throw them off, and we are not comfortable until we are undressed. In the same way, *"we that are in this tabernacle do groan, being burdened"* (2 Cor. 5:4). But when death frees the soul from the load and encumbrance of the body, which hinders its repose in its spiritual satisfactions, how light it will be! Let us think then of putting off the body at death with as much pleasure as we do of putting off our clothes at night. Let us be as unattached to it as we are to our clothes. Let us comfort ourselves with this thought: That though we are unclothed at death, if we are clothed with Christ and His grace, we will not be found naked but will be clothed with immortality. We have new clothes in the making, which will be ready to put on next morning, glorious bodies like Christ's instead of vile bodies like the animals have.

At death we will lie down in the grave as we lie down on our beds. We will lie down in the dust. To those who die in sin and unrepentance, the grave is a dungeon. Their iniquities that are upon their bones and that lie down with them (Job 20:11), make it so. But to those who die in Christ, who die in faith, it is a bed, a bed of rest, where they will not toss to and fro until dawn, as sometimes they do upon the most comfortable beds in this world. On that bed there is no danger of being scared with dreams or terrified with visions of the night. There is no being chastened with strong pain on that bed. It is the privilege of those who walk in their uprightness while they live to enter into peace and rest in their beds when they die (Isa. 57:2). Job comforted himself with this, in the midst of his agonies, that he would shortly make his bed in the darkness and be untroubled there. It is a bed of roses, a bed of spices, to all believers, ever since Jesus, who is the Rose of Sharon and the Lily of the Valleys, lay in it.

Say then of your grave, as you do of your bed at night, that there the weary are at rest. Take this further consolation: That you will not only rest there but soon rise from there, abundantly refreshed. You will be called up to meet the Beloved of your soul, to be forever with Him. You will rise to a day that will not renew your cares, as every day on earth does, but will secure to you unmixed and everlasting joys. How comfortably we may lie down at night if such thoughts as these lie down with us. How comfortably we may lie down at death if we have accustomed ourselves to such thoughts as these.

Confession of Daily Sins

Let us lie down with penitent reflections upon the sins of the day past. Praising God and delighting ourselves in Him is such pleasant work and so much the work of angels that it is a pity we should have anything else to do. But the truth is, we make other work for ourselves by our own folly that is not so pleasant but absolutely needful. That other work is repentance. At night, while we are solacing ourselves in God's goodness, we must mix with that the afflicting of ourselves for our own vileness. Both must have their places in us, and they will very well agree together.

We must be convinced that we are still contracting guilt. We carry corrupt natures around with us, which are bitter roots that bear gall and wormwood, and all we say or do is embittered by them. In many things we all offend (James 3:2), insomuch that there is not a just man upon earth who does good and does not sin (Eccl. 7:20). We are in the midst of a defiling world, and we cannot keep ourselves perfectly unspotted from it.

If we say we have no sin or that we have passed a day and have not sinned, we deceive ourselves (1 John 1:8). For if we know the truth, we will see cause to cry, *"Who can understand his errors?"* (Ps. 19:12). Cleanse us from our secret faults (v. 12), faults of which we ourselves are not aware. We ought to aim at a sinless perfection with as strict a watchfulness as if we could attain it. But, after all, we must acknowledge that we come short of it, that we have not yet attained, neither are already perfect. (See Philippians 3:12.) We find it by constant sad experience, for it is certain that we do enough every day to bring us to our knees at night.

We must examine our consciences so that we may find out our particular transgressions of the day past. Let us every night search and try our ways, thoughts, words, and actions. Let us compare them with the rule of the Word, examining our faces in that mirror so that we may see our spots and may be particular in the acknowledgment of them. It will be good for us to ask, What have I done today? What have I done wrong?

What duty have I neglected? What false step have I taken? How have I behaved in my calling, in my conversation? Have I done the duties demanded by my relationships? Have I submitted to the will of God in every event of providence? By doing this frequently, we will grow in our acquaintance with ourselves. Nothing will contribute more to our souls' prosperity.

We must renew our repentance for whatever we find has been amiss in us or has been said or done amiss by us. We must be sorry for it, sadly lament it, take shame to ourselves for it, and give glory to God by making confession. If anything appears to have been wrong more than ordinary, that must be particularly bewailed. In general, we must be mortified for our sins of daily weakness. We should not think slightly of them because they are returning daily. Rather, we should be the more ashamed of them and of the fountain within that casts out these waters.

It is good to be speedy in renewing our repentance before the heart is hardened by the deceitfulness of sin. Delays are dangerous. Fresh wounds may soon be cured, if caught in time. But if they are corrupt, as the psalmist said of his wounds in Psalm 38:5, it is our fault and folly, and the cure will be difficult. Though through the weakness of the flesh we fall into sin daily, if we get up again by renewed repentance at night, we are not utterly cast down nor should we think of ourselves as such. The sin that humbles us will not ruin us.

We must make a fresh application of the blood of Christ to our souls for the remission of our sins and for the gracious acceptance of our repentance. We must not think that we have need of Christ only at our first conversion to God. No, we have daily need of Him, as our Advocate with the Father. Therefore, as such, He always appears in the presence of God for us; He attends continually to this very thing. Even our sins of daily infirmity would be our ruin if He had not made satisfaction for them and did not still make intercession for us. He who is washed still needs to wash his feet from the filth he contracts in every step. And, blessed be God, there is a fountain opened for us to wash in, and it is always open.

We must make request at the throne of grace for peace and pardon. Those who repent must pray that the thoughts of their hearts may be forgiven them (Acts 8:22). And it is good to be particular in our prayers for the pardon of sin. As Hannah said concerning Samuel, *"For this child I prayed"* (1 Sam. 1:27), so we should be able to say, "For the forgiveness of this I prayed." However, the publican's prayer in general is a very proper one for each of us to lie down with: *"God be merciful to me a sinner"* (Luke 18:13).

Humble Prayers for Mercy

Let us lie down with humble supplications for the mercies of the night. Prayer is as necessary in the evening as it was in the morning, for we have the same need of the divine favor and care to make the evening to rejoice, as we had to beautify the morning.

We must pray that our outward man may be under the care of God's holy angels, who are the ministers of His providence. God has promised that He will give his angels charge concerning those who make the Most High their refuge (Ps. 91:9–11). The angels will pitch their tents round about them and deliver them. What God has promised we may and must pray for. It is not as if God needed the service of the angels, or as if He Himself quit all the care of His people and turned it over to the angels. However, it appears abundantly in Scripture that the angels, even though they are invisible, are employed around the people of God, whom He takes under His special protection. This is for the honor of God, by whom they are charged, and for the honor of the saints, with whom they are charged.

It was the glory of Solomon's bed that sixty of the most valiant men of Israel were around it, all holding swords because of fear in the night (Song 3:7–8). But much more honorably and comfortably are all true believers attended, for though they lie ever so lowly, they have hosts of angels surrounding their beds. By the ministration of good spirits they are preserved from malignant spirits. But God will *"for this be inquired of by the house of Israel"* (Ezek. 36:37). Christ Himself must pray the Father, and He will send to His relief legions of angels. (See Matthew 26:53.) Much more reason have we to ask, that it may be given us.

We must pray that our inward man may be under the influences of His Holy Spirit, who is the author and fountain of God's grace. Public ordinances are opportunities in which the Spirit works upon the hearts of men, and therefore when we attend them, we must pray for the Spirit's operations. Likewise is our retirement at night, and therefore we must offer the same prayer then.

We find that when people slumber upon their beds, God opens their ears and seals their instruction (Job 33:15–16). And with this, David's experience concurs. He found that God visited him in the night and tried him (Ps. 17:3). During the night God also gave him counsel, and his heart instructed him (Ps. 16:7); and so God revealed Himself to him. David found that nighttime was a proper season for remembering God and meditating on Him.

For the improvement of this proper season for conversing with God in solitude, we need the powerful and beneficial influences of the blessed

Spirit. Therefore, when we lie down, we should earnestly pray for His influences, humbly put ourselves under them, and submit ourselves to them. How God's grace may work on us when we are asleep we do not know. The soul will act in a state of separation from the body; and how far it acts independently on the body when the bodily senses are all locked up, we cannot say. But we are sure that the Spirit of the Lord is not bound.

We have reason to pray that our minds may not be disturbed or polluted by evil dreams, in which, for all we know, evil spirits sometimes have a hand. We should also pray that we may be instructed and quieted by good dreams. The Greek moralist Plutarch considered good dreams to be evidences of progress in virtue. To be sure, the good Spirit has an influence on our dreams. I have heard of a good man who used to pray at night for good dreams.

God certainly desires to hear our humble prayers for mercy. Let us pray to Him at the close of each day and receive His blessings.

Chapter 9

Heavenly Peace

I will...lay me down in peace.
—Psalm 4:8

When we lie down, our concern and endeavor must be to lie down in peace. It was promised to Abraham that he would go to his grave in peace. This promise is sure to all his spiritual seed, for the end of the upright man is peace (Ps. 37:37). Josiah died in peace, even though he was killed in a battle.

Now, as a pledge of this, let us every night lie down in peace. It is threatened to the wicked that they will *"lie down in sorrow"* (Isa. 50:11). It is promised to the righteous that they will lie down and none will make them afraid (Lev. 26:6). Let us then enter into this blessed rest and take care that we do not come short of it.

Let us lie down having peace with God, for without this there can be no peace at all. *"There is no peace, saith the LORD, unto the wicked"* (Isa. 48:22). God is at war with them. A state of sin is a state of enmity against God. They who continue in that state are under the wrath and curse of God and cannot lie down in peace. What do they have to do with peace? Hasten therefore sinner, hasten to make your peace with God in Jesus Christ, by repentance and faith. Take hold of His strength in order to make peace with Him, and you will make peace, for fury is not in Him.

Conditions of peace are offered; consent to them. Unite with Him who is our peace. Take Christ on His own terms, Christ on any terms. Do not delay to do this. Do not dare to go to sleep in that condition in which you do not dare to die. *"Escape for thy life; look not behind thee"* (Gen. 19:17). Acquaint yourself with Him right now, and be at peace. Thereby this good will come to you: You will lie down in peace.

Sin is at one time or another making mischief between God and our souls, provoking God against us, alienating us from God. We therefore need to make peace every night, reconciling ourselves to Him and to His holy will by the agency of His Spirit upon us and asking Him to be reconciled to us through the intercession of His Son for us. We want to have no distance, no strangeness, between us and God, no interposing cloud to hinder His mercies from coming down on us or our prayers from going up to Him. *"Being justified by faith, we have* [this] *peace with God through our Lord Jesus Christ"* (Rom. 5:1). Then we may not only lie down in peace, but we may *"rejoice in hope of the glory of God"* (v. 2). Let this be our first concern, that God have no quarrel with us, nor we with Him.

Let us lie down having peace with all men. It is in our best interests to go to sleep, as well as to die, in charity. Those who interact much with the world can scarcely go through a day without something or other happening that is provoking, some affront given to them, some injury done to them. Or at least they think so. When they retire at night and reflect on it, they are apt to magnify the offense. While they are musing on it, the fire burns, their resentments rise, and they begin to say, *"I will do so to him as he hath done to me"* (Prov. 24:29). Then follows a time of ripening the passion into a rooted malice and of meditating revenge.

Therefore, let wisdom and grace be put to work to extinguish this fire from hell before it gets ahead. Then let this root of bitterness be killed and plucked up. Let the mind be disposed to forgive the injury and to think well of, and wish well to, him who did it. If others are inclined to quarrel with us, let us resolve not to quarrel with them. Let us resolve that whatever the affront or injury is, it will neither disquiet our spirits nor make us fret, as Peninnah tried to do to Hannah. We must not let it sour or embitter our spirits or make us peevish and spiteful. Let us resolve to still love ourselves, and love our neighbor as ourselves, and therefore not do wrong to ourselves or our neighbor by harboring malice. We will find it much easier in itself, and much more pleasant in looking back, to forgive twenty injuries than to avenge one.

The charge in Ephesians 4:26 indicates that it should be our particular care at night to reconcile ourselves with those who have injured us: *"Let not the sun go down upon your wrath."* If your passion has not cooled before, let it be abated by the cool of the evening and allow it to quite disappear with the setting sun. You are then to go to bed, and if you lie down with these unmortified passions boiling in your breast, your soul is among lions; you lie down in a bed of thorns, in a nest of scorpions. Some have observed from the verse that immediately follows, *"Neither give place to the devil"* (v. 27), that those who go to bed in malice have the devil for their bedfellow.

We cannot lie down at peace with God unless we are at peace with men. We cannot pray in faith to be forgiven unless we forgive. Let us therefore study the things that make for peace, the peace of our own spirits, by living, as far as it depends on us, *"peaceably with all men"* (Rom. 12:18). *"I am for peace...*[though] *they are for war"* (Ps. 120:7).

Let us lie down in peace with ourselves, with our own minds, with a sweet composure of spirit and enjoyment of ourselves. *"Return unto thy rest, O my soul"* (Ps. 116:7), and be easy. Let nothing disturb my soul.

But when may we lie down in peace at night? If we have, by the grace of God, in some measure done the work of the day and filled the day with duty, we may then lie down in peace at night. If we have the testimony of our consciences that in simplicity and godly sincerity, not with fleshly wisdom, but by the grace of God, we have this day conducted ourselves in the world (2 Cor. 1:12), then we may lie down in peace. If we have done some good in our places, something that will turn to a good account, then we may lie down in peace. If our hearts do not reproach us with "Alas! I have wasted a day," or with what is even worse, spending our time in the service of sin instead of in the service of God, we may lie down in peace.

If we have abode with God, have been in His fear, and have waited on Him all the day long, we may then lie down in peace, for God says, *"Well done, good and faithful servant"* (Matt. 25:23). *"The sleep of a labouring man* [of a laboring Christian] *is sweet"* (Eccl. 5:12), very sweet, when he can say, "Just as I am a day's journey nearer my end, so I am a day's work fitter for it." Nothing will make our bedrooms pleasant and our beds comfortable like the witness of the Spirit of God with our spirits that we are going forward for heaven, as well as a conscience kept void of offense, which will be not only a continual feast but also a continual rest.

We may lie down in peace if we have, by faith and patience and submission to the divine will, reconciled ourselves to all the events of the day so as to be uneasy about nothing that God has done. Whatever unfortunate thing has happened to us, it should not fret us; but we will kiss the rod, take up the cross, and say, "All is well that God does." Thus we must, in our patience, keep possession of our own souls (Luke 21:19) and not allow any affliction to put us out of the possession of it.

Perhaps we have met with disappointments in our jobs. Perhaps debtors prove insolvent, or creditors prove severe. However, this and the other proceed from the Lord; there is a providence in it. Every creature is what God makes it to be, and therefore, I am silent; I will not open my mouth. That which pleases God ought not to displease me.

If we have renewed our repentance for sin and made a fresh application of the blood of Christ to our souls for the purifying of our consciences, we may then lie down in peace. Nothing can break in upon our peace but sin; that is what troubles the camp. If that is taken away, no evil will befall us. The inhabitant of Zion, though he is far from well, will not say, "I am sick," will not complain of sickness; for the people that dwell therein will be forgiven for their iniquities (Isa. 33:24). The pardon of sin has enough in it to balance all our griefs and therefore to silence all our complaints. A paralyzed man still has reason to be easy—no, to be of good cheer—if Christ says to him, *"Thy sins are forgiven thee"* (Luke 5:20), and, *"I am thy salvation"* (Ps. 35:3).

If we have put ourselves under the divine protection for the ensuing night, we may then lie down in peace. If, by faith and prayer, we have run into the name of the Lord as our strong tower, have fled to take shelter under the shadow of His wings, and have made the Lord our refuge and habitation, we may then speak peace to ourselves, for God in His Word speaks peace to us.

David, it is supposed, was thinking of the cherubim, between which God is said to dwell, when he said, *"In the shadow of thy wings will I make my refuge"* (Ps. 57:1). Yet, certainly, he had in mind the same metaphor that Christ used, of a hen gathering her chicks under her wings, when he said, *"He shall cover thee with his feathers, and under his wings shalt thou trust"* (Ps. 91:4). The chicks under the wings of the hen are not only safe but warm and pleased.

If we have cast all our cares concerning the next day on God, we may then lie down in peace. Worrying about the next day is the great hindrance of our peace in the night. Let us learn to live without disquieting care and to refer the outcome of all events to the God who may and can do what He will—and will do what is best for those who love and fear Him. Father, *"thy will be done"* (Matt. 6:10). When we give all things to Him, we make ourselves secure.

Our Savior emphasized this very much with His disciples, not to perplex themselves with thoughts about what they will eat and drink and how they will be clothed because their heavenly Father knows that they need these things and will see that they are supplied. Let us therefore ease ourselves of this burden by casting it on Him who cares for us. What need is there for Him to care and us to care, too?

Chapter 10

Bedtime Thoughts

*I will both lay me down in peace, and sleep:
for thou, LORD, only makest me
dwell in safety.*
—Psalm 4:8

Having laid ourselves down in peace, we must compose ourselves to sleep. *"I will both lay me down in peace, and sleep."* The love of sleep, for sleeping's sake, is the characteristic of the sluggard. But since sleep is nature's medicine for the replenishing of its weary powers, it is to be looked on as a mercy equal to that of our food and to be received in its season with thankfulness.

We should go to sleep with certain thoughts. The first is this: What poor bodies we have that call for rest and relief so often, that are so soon tired, even with doing nothing or next to nothing! Man is honored above the beasts in that he is made so erect. It was part of the serpent's curse that it would move on its belly. Yet we have little reason to boast of our honor when we observe how little a while we can stand upright, and how soon we are burdened with our honor and are forced to lie down.

The powers of the soul and the senses of the body are our honor, but it is humbling to consider how, after a few hours' use, they are all locked up and totally unable to act. It is necessary they should be so. *"Let not the wise man glory in his wisdom, neither let the mighty man glory in his might"* (Jer. 9:23), since they both lie for one fourth of their time utterly bereft of strength and wisdom and on a level with the weak and foolish.

Second, we should think about what a sad thing it is to be under the necessity of losing so much precious time in sleep! What a sad thing that we should lie so many hours out of every twenty-four, in no capacity at all of serving God or our neighbors, of doing any work of piety or charity! Those who consider how short our time is, what a great deal of work we have to do, and how fast the day of account hastens on, cannot but grudge to spend so much time in sleep. They wish to spend as little time as they can in sleep; they are quickened by sleep to redeem the time when they are awake. They long to be where there will be no need of sleep, where they will be like the angels of God and never rest day or night from the blessed work of praising God.

Third, we should think on our beds about what a good Master we serve, who allows us time for sleep and who furnishes us with the time and place for it. He also makes it refreshing and reviving to us. By this it appears that the Lord is for the body, and it is a good reason why we should present our bodies to Him as living sacrifices and glorify Him with them.

Sleep is given by promise to the saints. *"So he giveth his beloved sleep"* (Ps. 127:2). By a quiet resignation to God, the godly man has what the worldly man labors for in vain by the eager pursuit of the world. What a difference there is between the sleep of a sinner, who is not sensible of being within a step of hell, and the sleep of a saint, who has good hopes through grace of being within a step of heaven. That is the sleep God gives to His beloved.

Fourth, we should think about the pitiful case of those from whose eyes sleep departs, through pain of body or anguish of mind, and to whom wearisome nights are appointed. When they lie down, they say, "When will we arise?" They are thus made a terror to themselves. It was said that of all the inhuman tortures used by the French king to force his Protestant subjects to renounce their religion, none prevailed more than keeping them awake for long periods of time by violence. When we find how earnestly nature craves sleep and how much it is refreshed by it, we should think with compassion of those who, for any reason, lack that and other comforts that we enjoy, and we should pray for them.

We should consider, fifth, how ungrateful we have been to the God of our mercies in allowing sleep, which is so great a support and comfort to us, to be our hindrance in that which is good. We should consider the times when sleep has been the gratification of our sloth and laziness, when it has kept us from our hour of prayer in the morning and unfitted us for our hour of prayer at night. Call to mind the times you have slept unseasonably in the worship of God, as Eutychus did when Paul was preaching; and the disciples, when Christ was in His agony at prayer. How just it would be if we were deprived of the comfort of sleep and reproved with this as the provoking cause of it! *"What, could ye not watch with me one hour?"* (Matt. 26:40). Those who want to sleep, and cannot, must think of how often they should have kept awake, and would not.

We have now one day less to live than we had in the morning. The thread of time is winding off quickly; its sands are running down. As time goes, eternity comes. It is hastening on. Our days are swifter than a weaver's shuttle, which passes and repasses in an instant. What are we doing with our time? Are we cheerfully ready to give an account? Oh, that we could always go to sleep with death in our thoughts. How it would quicken us to improve our use of time! It would not make our sleep the less desirable, but it would make our deaths much less formidable.

As we go to sleep, we should say, "To Your glory, O God, I now go to sleep." Whether we eat or drink, yes, or sleep, for that is included in *"whatsoever ye do"* (1 Cor. 10:31), we must do it to the glory of God. Why do I go to sleep now except that my body may be fit to serve my soul and able for a while to keep pace with it in the service of God tomorrow? Common actions, performed with our great goal in mind, are done after a godly sort and abound to our account; and thus the advantages we have by them are sanctified to us. *"Unto the pure all things are pure"* (Titus 1:15). And *"whether we wake or sleep, we should live together with him* [Christ]" (1 Thess. 5:10).

We should say, as we go to sleep, "To Your grace, O God, and to the word of Your grace, I now commend myself." It is good to fall asleep with a fresh surrender of our whole selves—body, soul, and spirit—to God. *"Return unto thy rest* [which is

God], *O my soul; for the* LORD *hath dealt bountifully with thee"* (Ps. 116:7). Thus, when we are falling asleep, we should commit the keeping of our souls to Him as David did, saying, *"Into thine hand I commit my spirit"* (Ps. 31:5); and as Stephen did, with, *"Lord Jesus, receive my spirit"* (Acts 7:59).

Sleep not only resembles death, but it is also sometimes an inlet to it. Many go to sleep and never wake; they sleep the sleep of death. This is a good reason why we should go to sleep with dying thoughts and put ourselves under the protection of a living God, and then sudden death will be no surprise to us.

Oh, when I awake may I still be with God! May the parenthesis of sleep, though long, not break off the thread of my communion with God. As soon as I awake, may I resume it! Oh, that when I wake in the night I may have my mind turned to good thoughts! May I remember God upon my bed, who then is at my right hand and to whom the daytime and the nighttime are both alike. Oh, that I may sweetly meditate on Him in the night watches. Then even that time will be redeemed and improved to the best advantage, which otherwise is in danger not only of being lost in vain thoughts but misspent in wrong ones! Oh, that when I awake in the morning my first thoughts may be of God, that with them my heart may be seasoned for the entire day!

Bedtime Thoughts

Oh, that I may enter into a better rest than that which I am now entering into! The apostle speaks of a rest that we who have believed do enter into, even in this world. He also speaks of a rest that remains in the other world for the people of God. Believers rest from sin and the world; they rest in Christ and in God through Christ. They enjoy a satisfaction in the covenant of grace. This is my rest forever; here will I dwell. They enter into this ark, and there they are not only safe but also peaceful. Oh, that I might enjoy this rest while I live; and when I die, may I enter into something more than rest, even the joy of my Lord, a fullness of joy!

Dependence on a Faithful God

We must do all this in a believing dependence on God and His power, providence, and grace. Therefore, I lie down in peace and sleep, because You, Lord, keep me, and assure me that You do so. *"Thou, Lord...makest me dwell in safety."* David took notice of God's notice, for God noticed his path and his lying down (Ps. 139:3). God was his observer. David saw God's eye upon him when he was retiring into his bedroom and no one else saw him, when he was in the dark and no one else saw him. Here God took notice of him, watching his lying down as his Preserver. David saw God's hand on him to protect him from evil and to keep him safe. He felt His hand under him to support him and to make him calm.

It is by the power of God's providence that we are kept safe in the night, and on that providence we must depend continually. It is He who preserves man and beast (Ps. 36:6), who upholds all things by the word of His power (Heb. 1:3). Death, which by sin entered into the world, would soon lay all to waste if God did not shelter His creatures from its arrows.

Death's arrows are continually flying about, and we cannot help but feel exposed to them in the night. Our bodies carry around with them the seeds of all diseases. Death is always working in us. A little thing would stop the circulation either of the blood or the breath, and then we are gone; either we will never awake, or we will awake under the arrests of death. Men by sin are exposed to one another. Many have been murdered in their beds, and many burned in their beds. And our greatest danger of all is from the malice of evil spirits, which go about seeking to devour.

We are very much unable to help ourselves, and our friends are unable to help us. We are not aware of the particulars of our danger, nor can we foresee which way it will arise. Therefore, we do not know where to stand on guard, or, if we did, we do not know how. When Saul was asleep, he lost his spear and his jug of water, and he might as easily have lost his head. Sisera lost his head by the hand of a woman when he was asleep. What poor, helpless creatures we are, and how easily we are overcome when sleep has overcome us! Our friends are asleep, too, and cannot help us. An illness may seize us in the night, and, even if they are called and come to us, they may not be able to help us. The most skillful and tender care may be of no value.

It is therefore God's providence that protects us night after night, His care, His goodness. That was the hedge around Job, around him, his house, and all that he had (Job 1:10). This was a hedge that Satan himself could not break through, or find a gap in, though he wandered around it. There is a special protection that God's people are taken under. They are hidden *"in his pavilion: in the secret of his tabernacle"* (Ps. 27:5), under the protection of His promise. They are His own and dear to Him; He keeps them as the apple of His eye (Ps. 17:8). He is round about them from this time forth and forever, *"as the mountains are round about Jerusalem"* (Ps. 125:2).

He protects their habitations as He did the tents of Israel in the wilderness. He has promised to create upon every dwelling place of Mount Zion *"a cloud...by day,"* to shelter from heat, and *"the shining of a flaming fire by night"* (Isa. 4:5), to shelter from cold. Thus He blesses the habitation of the just so that no real evil will befall it and no plague will come near it.

We are to depend on the care of divine providence over us and our families. We must not look on any provision we make for our own safety as sufficient without the blessing of the divine providence upon it. *"Except the LORD keep the city, the watchman waketh but in vain"* (Ps. 127:1). Be the house ever so well built, the doors and windows ever so well barred, the servants ever so watchful, it is all to no purpose unless He who keeps Israel and neither slumbers nor sleeps undertakes for our safety. If He is your protector, *"at destruction and famine thou shalt laugh"* (Job 5:22), and *"thou shalt know that thy tabernacle* [is] *in peace"* (Job 5:24).

It is by the power of God's grace that we are enabled to think ourselves safe, and on that grace we must continually depend. The fear of danger, though groundless, is as vexatious as if it were ever so justified. And therefore to complete the mercy of being made to dwell safely, it is necessary that by the grace of God we be delivered from our fears as well as from the things themselves that we are afraid of. In this way, shadows will not be a terror to us, nor will substantial evils.

If, by God's grace, we are enabled to keep clear consciences and preserve our integrity, if iniquity is put far away and no wickedness allowed to dwell in our homes, then we will lift up our faces without spot; we will be steadfast and will not need to fear (Job 11:14–15). For fear came in with sin and goes out with it. If our hearts do not condemn us, then we have confidence toward God and man, too. We are made to dwell securely, for we are sure nothing can hurt us but sin. Whatever does harm us, sin is the sting of it. Therefore, if sin is pardoned and prevented, we do not need to fear any trouble.

The grace of God enables us to live by faith. Faith sets God always before us. Faith applies the promises to ourselves and brings petitions to the throne of grace. Faith purifies the heart, overcomes the world, and quenches all the fiery darts of the Wicked One. Faith realizes unseen things and is the substance and evidence of them.

If we are enabled to live by this faith, we are made to dwell safely. We can bid defiance to death itself and all its harbingers and terrors. *O death, where is thy sting?* (1 Cor. 15:55). This faith will not only silence our fears but will also open our lips in holy triumphs. *If God be for us, who can be against us?* (Rom. 8:31).

Let us lie down in peace and sleep, not by resolving in our own strength not to fear nor by using rational arguments against fear, though they are of good use, but in a dependence on the grace of God to work faith in us and to fulfill in us the work of faith. This is going to sleep like a Christian under the shadow of God's wings, going to sleep in faith. It will be to us a good pledge of dying in faith, for the same faith that will carry us cheerfully through the short death of sleep will carry us through the long sleep of death.

A Life of Secret Communion

We should carry our religion with us wherever we go and have it always at our right hand. For at every turn we have occasion for it, lying down, rising up, going out, and coming in. They are Christians indeed who do not confine their religion to religious holidays and Sundays but bring the influences of it into all the common actions and occurrences of human life. We must sit down at our tables and rise from them, lie down on our beds and arise from them, with our eyes on God's providence and promise. Thus we must live a life of communion with God, even while we conduct ourselves in the world.

In order for this to happen, it is necessary that we have a living principle in our hearts, a principle of grace, which, like a well of living water, may continually spring up to life eternal (John 4:14). It is likewise necessary that we watch our hearts and keep them with all diligence. We must set a strict guard upon our hearts' actions and have our thoughts more at command than, I fear, most Christians have. Take note of our great need of the constant supplies of divine grace and of a union with Christ, so that by faith we may partake of the root and fatness of the good olive tree continually (Rom. 11:17).

See what a hidden life the life of a good Christian is and how much it is concealed from the eye and observation of the world. The most important part of the business lies between God and our own souls, in the frame of our spirits and the workings of our hearts, in our actions that no eye sees except the all-seeing God. Justly are the saints called God's hidden ones, and His secret is said to be with them. They have meat to eat and work to do that the world does not know of, as well as joys, griefs, and cares that a stranger does not share. *"Great is the mystery of godliness"* (1 Tim. 3:16).

And this is a good reason why we are incompetent to judge one another, because we do not know each other's hearts and we are not witnesses to each other's private actions. It is to be feared that there are many whose religion lies all on the outside. They make a good impression, and perhaps a great noise, and yet are strangers to this secret communion with God, in which so much of the power of godliness consists.

On the other hand, it is to be hoped that there are many who do not distinguish themselves by anything observable in their Christian walk, but pass through the world without being taken notice of and yet converse with God in solitude and walk with Him in regular devotion. *"The kingdom of God cometh not with observation"* (Luke 17:20). Many merchants thrive by a secret trade and make no bustle in the world. It is fit therefore that every man's judgment should proceed from the Lord, who knows men's hearts and sees in secret.

What enemies they are to themselves who continue under the power of a vain and carnal mind and live without God in the world. I fear that there are multitudes to whom all that has been said of secret communion with God is accounted as a strange thing, and they say of their ministers when they speak of it, "Do they not speak parables?" (See Ezekiel 20:49.) They lie down and rise up, go out and come in, in the constant pursuit either of worldly profits or of sensual pleasures. But God is not in all their thoughts, not in any of them. They live upon Him and upon the gifts of His bounty from day to day, but they have no regard for Him, never acknowledge their dependence on Him, nor are at all concerned to secure His favor.

Those who live such a mere animal life as this, not only show a great contempt for God but also do a great deal of damage to themselves. They stand in the way of their own light, and they deprive themselves of the most valuable comforts that can be enjoyed on this side of heaven. Those who are not at peace with God, what peace can they have? Those who do not build their hopes on God, who is the everlasting foundation, what hope can they have? Those who do not derive their joy from God, who is the fountain of life and living waters, what true joy can they have? Oh, that at length they would be wise for themselves and remember their Creator and benefactor!

What easy, pleasant lives the people of God might live if it were not for their own faults. There are those who fear God, work righteousness, and are accepted by the Lord, but go drooping and disconsolate from day to day, are full of cares, fears, and complaints, and make themselves always fretful. It is because they do not live that life of delight in God and dependence on Him that they might and should live. God has effectually provided for their dwelling at ease, but they do not make use of that provision He has laid up for them.

Oh, that all who appear to be conscientious and are afraid of sin would appear to be cheerful and afraid of nothing else. May all who call God Father, who are careful to please Him, and who keep themselves in His love learn to cast all their other cares upon Him and commit their ways to Him as to a father. He will choose our inheritances for us, and He knows what is best for us better than we do for ourselves. It is what I have often said and will abide by, that a holy, heavenly life, spent in the service of God and in communion with Him, is the most pleasant, comfortable life anybody can live in this world.

Consider the best preparation we can make for the changes that may be before us: We must keep up a constant acquaintance and communion with God, converse with Him daily, and keep up stated times for calling on Him, so that when trouble comes it may find the wheels of prayer going. Then may we come to God with a humble boldness and comfort. Then we can speed to Him when we are in affliction, for we have not been strangers to Him at other times but, in our peace and prosperity, have had our eyes ever toward Him.

Even when we arrive at the greatest degree of holy security and serenity and lie down most in peace, still we must keep up an expectation of trouble in the flesh. Our peace must not be grounded upon any stability in any person or thing. If it is, we cheat ourselves and treasure up greater vexation for ourselves. No, it must be built upon the faithfulness of God, who is unchangeable. Our Master has told us, "'In the world ye shall have tribulation' (John 16:33), much tribulation; count on it. It is only in Me that you will have peace." But if every day is to us as it should be—a sabbath of rest in God and communion with Him—nothing can come amiss to us any day, be it ever so undesirable.

We should consider what is the best preparation we can make for the unchangeable world that is before us. We know God will bring us to death, and it is our great concern to get ready for it. It ought to be the business of every day to prepare for our last day. What can we do better for ourselves in the prospect of death than, by frequent times of communion with God, become less attached to the world that at death we must leave and better acquainted with the world that at death we must go to? By going to our beds as to our graves, we will make death familiar to us, and it will become as easy for us to close our eyes in peace and die as it used to be to close our eyes in peace and sleep.

We hope God will bring us to heaven, and by keeping up daily communion with God, we grow more and more fit to partake of that inheritance and have our citizenship in heaven. It is certain that all who will go to heaven hereafter begin their heaven now and have their hearts there. If we thus enter into a spiritual rest every night, that will be a pledge of our blessed repose in the embraces of divine love, in that world wherein day and night come to an end. There we will not rest day or night from praising Him who is and will be our eternal rest.

Chapter 11

Harmful Communication

*Let no corrupt communication proceed out
of your mouth, but that which is good to the
use of edifying, that it may minister
grace unto the hearers.*
—Ephesians 4:29

Like other common actions of life, that of visiting our friends should be done in a godly manner. To assist you in this, I will offer some words of caution against those things that corrupt our visits and turn them into sin. And by way of direction, I will point out those things that will sanctify our visits and make them fulfill a very good purpose.

Be careful that your visits to your friends and your questions about their welfare do not cause harm. We must not decide if this is the case by using the common sentiment or fashion of a vain world; for our Savior has told us that what is highly esteemed among men, perhaps as a mighty accomplishment or a part of very good upbringing, can be an abomination in the sight of God (Luke 16:15). Let us therefore have recourse to the Bible and take admonition from there in this case.

Let us be careful that our friendly visits are not a waste of our precious time. We are entrusted with time as a talent to be traded with for eternity. As we spend our time well or ill, so will our eternity be spent, comfortably or miserably. Every good Christian will therefore endeavor to be a good steward of his time. Good stewardship is good theology. It is not only necessary to spend part of our time in actual preparation for another world, but all our time must be spent with a habitual regard to it. Every hour of the worker's workday must be at the disposal of the one who hired him. Our time is not our own, for we know in whose hands our times are, and we must always live for Him, by whom we always live.

God's wisdom will therefore direct us as to what proportion of time is to be allotted to every service, both of our general and particular callings. In this way, our various duties and our various enjoyments will not interfere with one another. Everything is beautiful in its season. To every purpose there is a time, which the wise man's heart discerns. Now, if time is spent in visits that should be spent in any duties necessary to life or godliness, then they are not Christian visits. If, under the pretense of visiting friends, we indulge ourselves in sloth and laziness and carelessly neglect business and labor, we will give a bad account of so many hours misspent.

We may justly say to many, as Pharaoh unjustly said to Moses and the Israelites, *"Ye are idle, ye are idle: therefore ye say, Let us go"* (Exod. 5:17). The apostle described people like this: *"They learn to be idle, wandering about from house to house"* (1 Tim. 5:13). They go from house to house under the pretense of friendly visits. Not only are they idle, they are *"tattlers also and busybodies"* (v. 13). For few who are idle are only idle; usually they have other faults. When they have nothing to do, the devil will find them something to do. They are idle in good but busy in evil. But what will they do when God rises up and brings them into judgment for all their idle visits, idle frolics, and every idle word?

Learn therefore to adjust the use of your time, and do not be wasteful of such a talent. When you say that you will go and visit a friend, ask, "Can I afford time for it? Is there not some greater good to be done at the same time, which cannot so well be deferred until another time? Will my calling not be neglected or some religious duties be prevented by it?" The thing that is most necessary should be done first, and let everything be done in its own order. When a visit that must be made takes time away from other business, we would be wise to carefully use the visit for some very good purpose so that we may at least save it from being an idle visit.

Let us take heed that our friendly visits are not the gratifications of pride and vain curiosity. Those who *"desire to make a fair show in the flesh"* (Gal. 6:12) visit their friends only to see and be seen. They want to show themselves in their best ornaments and accomplishments and observe what appearance other people make and what they distinguish themselves by. They go abroad only to learn fashions and to see how the world goes.

They are like the Athenians, who spent their time in nothing else but either telling or hearing something new (Acts 17:21), or like Dinah, who went out to see the daughters of the land (Gen. 34:1), to see how they were dressed, what entertainments they gave, and how they lived. She only wanted something to talk about when she came home, either by way of praise or censure. This was her only business, and the sequel of the story shows that the journey was not for her honor. Yet it is to be feared that many of our visits are made from no better a principle.

Decency indeed is duty. Civility must be paid and returned according to the current custom of our country. Religion was never intended to destroy good manners or to make people rude and unfashionable. But in our compliances with the customs of our country and acquaintances, we need to look well to our spirits and keep our hearts with all diligence. We must be careful that the action that is innocent and commendable in itself does not arise from a corrupt motive and so become sin to us.

Hezekiah's showing his house, furniture, armory, and jewels to the Babylonian king's ambassadors seemed but a token of common respect and what is usually done among friends. Yet, because he did it in the pride of his heart, wrath came upon him and on Judah and Jerusalem. This is recorded as a warning to all. Even those who have escaped the grosser corruptions that are in the world through lust must take heed lest foolish pride make their visits, dress, and compliments a snare to them.

Pride is a subtle sin, a sin that easily besets us, a sin that is apt to mingle itself with our best actions. Like a dead fly, it spoils many a pot of precious ointment. We therefore need to keep a jealous eye and a strict hand upon the actions of our own souls in this business of making and receiving visits. We must be careful *lest being lifted up with pride* [we] *fall into the condemnation of the devil*" (1 Tim. 3:6).

If, in our common conversations, we are more eager to approve ourselves to men by appearing happy and agreeable than to approve ourselves to God, either by doing or getting good, surely we forget the fundamental law of Christianity: *"They which live should not henceforth live unto themselves, but unto him which died for them, and rose again"* (2 Cor. 5:15). Unfortunately, there is a common principle that too many govern themselves by more than by the principles of religion: "It is as good to be out of the world as to be out of fashion." This saying, however, ought to have no sway with those who know that they are called out of the world, and are not to be conformed to it, nor are to walk according to the course of it.

Even while we accommodate ourselves to the fashions of our country and of our places in it, we should always endeavor to be dead to them and to observe them with a holy indifference. We are to act as those who seek a better country, that is, a heavenly country, and who belong to it. We may do what others do, yet not in the same way that most do it. Let the visits we make daily to our God in prayer be more our concern, and more our delight, than any visits we make to our friends.

Let us take heed that our friendly visits are not the cloak and concealment of hypocrisy. Let them not be like the visits David's enemies made to him. David said of his enemy: *"If he come to see me, he speaketh vanity"* (Ps. 41:6); that is, what he says by way of compassion and condolence is all counterfeit and pretended. *"His heart gathereth iniquity to itself; when he goeth abroad, he telleth it"* (v. 6). This is an evil practice, and one that all who have any sense of virtue and honor will cry out against. Next to hypocrisy in religion, nothing is worse than hypocrisy in friendship.

It is bad enough if kindness is not intended in our visits and if we do not truly respect those whom we claim to respect. Love ought to be without hypocrisy. But it is much worse if mischief and unkindness are intended to those to whom we pretend to make visits of friendship. It is sinful if we go to see them in order to find something against them and to pick up something to bring them reproach in our next discussions. To make the ceremonies of friendship serve the designs of malice is to involve ourselves in a double guilt, both the lack of love and the lack of sincerity.

This does not mean that if you are displeased with someone to whom you owe respect that you must instantly break off all interaction and conversation with him and deny due civilities to him for fear of hypocrisy. No, that will make the matter worse. But you must mortify the corrupt passion that is working in you. You must not let the sun go down on your wrath. You must forgive the injury, whether real or imaginary. You must be reconciled to your friend, cordially reconciled, and then come and offer your gift to God and your respects to your friend. We ought to carefully avoid everything that tends to alienate the affections of Christians one from another and to cool love. We ought to devise all means possible for the preservation of true friendship where it exists and the reparation and retrieval of it where it is withering and ready to die.

Let us take heed that our friendly visits do not become opportunities for slandering and gossiping. Our rule is: Speak evil of no man. By evil, I mean not only what is false and altogether groundless but also what is true, when our speaking of it will do more harm than good. If we are unable to speak well of those we talk about, we had better not say anything about them at all. The general law of justice obliges us to treat others as we want to be treated. We would not want our own faults and follies, our own miscarriages and mismanagements, proclaimed in all companies and made the subject of discourse and remark. Let us then treat other people's good names with the same tenderness that we expect and desire our own to be treated with.

There is also a particular law of love that obliges us to cover even a multitude of sins, to keep secret that which is secret. For we do not need to make scandals by divulging that which could be concealed. As for that which cannot be hidden, we must speak of it as those who mourn and not as those who are proud. We should be willing to make the best, and hope the best, of every person and every action. We must not act as if we were prosecuting a delinquent. We must not think ourselves obliged to magnify the crime and press for judgment against the criminal.

Nothing is more destructive to love and friendship than gossip. In the Scriptures we have laws against it: *"Thou shalt not go up and down as a talebearer* [gossiper] *among thy people"* (Lev. 19:16). The word used here and elsewhere for a talebearer signifies a peddler who buys goods (stolen ones, it may be) at one place and sells them at another. So a talebearer makes his visits to pick up at one place and to utter at another that which he thinks will lessen his neighbor's reputation, so that he may build his own upon the ruin of it.

We have another law to the same effect: *"Thou shalt not raise a false report"* (Exod. 23:1). This also means, "Thou shalt not receive a false report." Many times, the receiver in this case is as bad as the thief. We also have proverbs against gossip, or talebearing. *"He that goeth about* [making visits, for instance] *as a talebearer revealeth secrets"* (Prov. 20:19). *"Where there is no talebearer, the strife ceaseth"* (Prov. 26:20). *"The words of a talebearer are as wounds"* (v. 22).

Those who make it their business in their visits to carry critical, ill-natured stories from place to place wound their neighbor's good name secretly, propagate contempts and jealousies, and sow discord. They do the devil's work and serve his interests more than they realize. That great and good man, St. Augustine, ordered the law of his house to be written over his table, giving gossips no room there: "Be it known that this table is forbidden the man who delights in injuring the reputation of absent persons." David, one greater than he, did the same thing: *Whoso privily slandereth his neighbour, him will I cut off* (Ps. 101:5). I heartily wish that not the people who slander, but the slander itself, would be cut off from all conversation.

Chapter 12

Helpful Hospitality

Let your speech be alway with grace,
seasoned with salt, that ye may know
how ye ought to answer every man.
—Colossians 4:6

Allow, I entreat you, a word of counsel and direction. Let us all endeavor to serve some good purpose in our visits to our friends and in our questions about their welfare. May our visits not only be rectified and made innocent, but sanctified and made excellent. May they be managed so as to rescue them from being lost time, which too many of our visits have been.

Even acts of civility may be so improved that they become acts of piety. Also, the common greeting, "How are you doing?" may, by a good intention, be advanced to the rank of good words. Those who fear the Lord speak good words often to one another, and the Lord pays attention and hears and writes them in a book of remembrance (Mal. 3:16). When the sincere, sacred words of "God be with you" and "God bless you" are used carelessly and lightly, they degenerate and turn into the sin of taking the name of the Lord in vain. Even so, these common greetings, "How are you doing?" and "How is your family?" may be consecrated by a motive of Christian friendship, and we may even glorify God through them.

Much of what I am saying about personal visits to our friends may also be applied to our friendly letters. We ought to keep up our correspondence with pure motives and in a Christian manner, so that we may not have to answer for wasted paper, as well as lost time. Let us then follow these same directions in our letters as we do in our visits.

Let our friendly visits be the proofs and preservatives of brotherly love. Brotherly love is the law of Christ's kingdom, the emblem of His family, the great lesson to be learned in His school. Nothing is more the beauty and strength of the Christian church, or a brighter ornament to the holy religion that we profess. It is maintained by reciprocal kindnesses and particularly by mutual visits. Our intention must be to love therefore both in giving and receiving visits.

We must manage our visits accordingly, to testify our affection toward those to whom we are obliged, by nature, providence, or grace—to respect, and so to show the proof of our love. Our godly visits confirm and improve that unity in which believers ought to dwell together. We must therefore visit one another, so that we may the better love one another, with a pure heart, and more fervently.

Mutual strangeness and unnatural distance are both the effects and the causes of the decay of love. They are evidences that love is cooled, and they cool it yet more, perhaps by degrees killing it. They give Satan room to sow his tares. When relatives and neighbors and friends are as shy of one another and as reserved as if they had never seen one another before in this world, and never expected to see one another in a better world, it is easy to say, contrary to what was said of the early Christians, "See how little these people love one another." But when they visit each other with mutual freeness and openness, embrace each other with a cordial affection, and concern themselves with each other with all possible tenderness, by this it will appear that they are taught by God to love one another. Hereby the holy fire is kept burning upon the altar.

Since our lots are cast in those latter days in which it is foretold that iniquity will abound, and the love of many wax cold (Matt. 24:12), those perilous times in which men will be lovers of themselves only (2 Tim. 3:1–2), it is a good service to the public to cultivate true and hearty friendship by all means possible. Why should we be strangers to one another, we who hope to be together forever with the Lord?

The diseases of selfishness and deceit may prove obstinate to these methods of cure. Yet, if we prove ourselves warm and cordial in our love, we will have the comfort of having done our duty and having delivered our souls. Perhaps they who are more loving than others will have the further comfort of being better beloved than others, for he who waters will also be watered himself (Prov. 11:25).

Let our friendly visits be the helps and occasions of Christian sympathy. Christian sympathy is one branch of Christian love. As it is in the natural body, so it ought to be in Christ's body: *"Whether one member suffer, all the members suffer with it; or one member be honoured, all the members rejoice with it"* (1 Cor. 12:26). What is love but a union of souls and an intertwining of interests? And where these are, there will be sympathy, according to that law of our religion, *"Rejoice with them that do rejoice, and weep with them that weep"* (Rom. 12:15).

We must therefore visit our friends and see how they are doing, so that we may rejoice with them in those things that cause them to rejoice. When we find them and their families in health and peace, their jobs successful, their income increased, their relationships happy, we may be comforted in their comfort. God takes pleasure in the prosperity of His servants (Ps. 35:27), and so should we. And we should be the more conscientious to show ourselves pleased in the prosperity of our friends because most seek their own welfare and few another's welfare; from this arise envy and mutual jealousies.

We must likewise desire to know the state of our friends so that we may mourn with them for their afflictions and mingle our tears with theirs. If the hand of the Lord is gone out against them and damage is done to them and their comforts, we may give them some relief. We can show them goodwill in their sorrows and assure them of our continued friendship when they are most apt to be discouraged and to think themselves slighted. Also, giving them an opportunity to share their troubles with someone who will listen to them, not only with patience but also with tenderness and compassion, gives some ease to a burdened spirit. Perhaps we may then speak some word in season, which God may bless for the strengthening of weak hands and feeble knees.

On this errand Job's friends came to visit him when they heard of all the evil that had come upon him. They came *"to mourn with him and to comfort him"* (Job 2:11). It is some comfort to mourners to have their friends mourn with them. Thus Nehemiah asked about the condition of his friends with a tender concern, as we see by his deep resentment of the evil tidings brought to him: "[He] *sat down and wept, and mourned certain days"* (Neh. 1:4). Let us learn in this manner to bear one another's burdens by a compassionate sorrow for others' griefs. This secondhand suffering will either prevent our own afflictions or prepare us for them.

Let our friendly visits furnish us with matter for prayer and praise. Besides the hint that our Master has given us in teaching us to address ourselves to God as our Father, we have an express command: *"Pray one for another"* (James 5:16). It our duty likewise to give thanks for one another, for whenever a mercy that we have prayed for is given, we ought to return thanks for it.

We find Paul, in most of his epistles, both to churches and particular friends, speaking of the prayers and thanksgivings he offered up to God daily upon their account. No doubt it was an unspeakable comfort to them to think of the interest they had in the prayers of so great an intercessor as Paul. It is written also for our learning, that we may in like manner give thanks to God for our friends, making mention of them always in our prayers. This will show our affection for them and make us truly serviceable to their comfort, when perhaps we are not in a capacity of being so any other way. Thus we may keep up the communion of saints in faith, hope, and love.

It is good to visit our fellow believers and to see how they are doing so that we may pray for others more particularly and more sensibly. The subject of their rejoicing, and ours with them, we may make the subject of our thanksgiving to God. Whatever just complaint they make to us, we may with them spread it before the Lord and beg relief and comfort for them. When we visit our friends, we have an opportunity to pray with them; and I heartily wish it were more practiced, especially by ministers. This would indeed sanctify our visits and turn them to a very good account.

When you are sick and in trouble, you desire someone to pray with you. Why should you not desire someone to pray with you when you are in health and peace? A Christian friend may pray for your prosperity to be continued and sanctified and for you to be kept from the snares and temptations of it. Likewise, help in returning thanks is as necessary as help in prayer. Those who know how to properly value the privilege of communion with God will reckon this as good an enjoyment as they can either give or receive.

Besides the opportunity that visiting gives of praying together, it gives us much assistance in praying for one another when we are alone. When we have seen our friends and talked with them, or when we have heard from them, we can pray the more affectionately for them. There is a rule that you may find helpful. (However, I ask you to mind conscience, not bind it.) The rule is this: Those friends whom in the day we have visited, or have visited us, whom we have written to, or heard from, we should at night in our prayer closets particularly pray for and give thanks for, as there is occasion. I do not know why we may not spread the letter of a friend before the Lord, as Hezekiah did the letter of an enemy.

Some have observed that they have had the most comfort from those relatives and friends whom they have prayed for the most. However, if we are disappointed, as David was, because those we pray for prove unkind to us, it will be our satisfaction as it was his, that our prayers will return into our own bosoms (Ps. 35:13), and we ourselves will have the comfort of them.

The following is a pious request that serious Christians commonly make to one another, both by word and letter: "Remember me in your prayers." It is good to use it, provided it does not degenerate into a formality. Our requests for prayer should come from a deep sense of our own needs and unworthiness, a real value both for the duty of prayer in general and for our friends and their prayers in particular. Of course, I am speaking of those friends who have an interest in heaven.

Christians are separated from each other in this scattering world; it is a world we cannot always expect to be together in. Yet, by our mutual requests for a share in each other's prayers, we make appointments for meeting often at the same throne of grace in hopes of meeting soon at the right hand of the throne of glory to part no more.

Let us improve our friendly visits. Let us use them as opportunities for doing good to the souls of our friends. Spiritual charity, though it must begin at home in teaching ourselves and our families, must not end there. We must contribute what we can to the edification of others in knowledge, faith, holiness, and joy. This is a mutual duty to be studied and done in giving and receiving visits. As iron sharpens iron, so our pious affections and resolutions may be sharpened by conversation with one another (Prov. 27:17).

We are often commanded to exhort one another, admonish one another, teach one another, comfort one another, and stir up one another to that which is good. And when can this be better done than when we come together for mutual society? Then we have a payment put into our hands, if we simply have a heart to use it, if we have the skill, will, and courage to make it profitable.

Much has been said, and much written, to promote godly discourse among Christians, but I fear it has done little good. We all have reason to lament that so much corrupt communication comes out of our mouths. We say so little that is good and edifying, so little that might manifest grace in him who speaks or minister grace to them who hear. *"Shall vain words have an end?"* (Job 16:3). Will we always use unprofitable talk and speeches that do no good but are in danger of doing harm? Will we never learn the art of introducing and keeping up profitable discourse in our conversations with our friends? Will we never learn to use words that we will be able to recall with comfort on that Day of Judgment, when by our words we must be justified and by our words we must be condemned (Matt. 12:37)? A visit thus improved will be fruit abounding to a good account.

Through godly conversation, you may help save a soul from death, eternal death, or at least further a soul toward eternal life. Thus we must confess Christ before men, as those who are not ashamed of Him or His words. Reproach for it we must not fear. We can boldly say, "If this is esteemed to be vile, *'I will yet be more vile'* (2 Sam. 6:22)." No, we do not need to fear. Perhaps even the very people whose reproach we fear, if we manage their scorn with meekness and humility and without pretense, may hold us in honor. Serious godliness is a powerful thing, and it will command respect.

I grant that our discourses with our friends cannot be turned entirely into this channel. Allowance must be made for a great deal of common talk. Yet even upon that there should appear an air of religion and godliness. Though a foreigner may speak English, ordinarily we can discern by his pronunciation that he is a foreigner. So, though a good Christian cannot avoid speaking much of the things of this world, he should speak in such a way that those he talks with may note that he belongs to another world and has been with Jesus. Then they may say to him, "You are a Christian, for your speech gives you away."

The great Mr. Boyle was observed never to mention the name of God without a discerning pause, or stop, leaving room for a pious thought. If we also speak of God and His providence with reverence and a holy awe, if we follow our consciences in what we say, if we are afraid of offending with our lips, if the law of kindness is in our tongues, if we speak of common things in a godly way, God will be honored and our lives will be beautified. Those we converse with will be edified and will say that God is truly with us. Our speech, though it is not always *of* grace, should always be *with* grace, seasoned with it as with salt, which gives it its own relish and flavor.

Let our friendly visits be opportunities for getting good for our own souls. By doing good, we do indeed get good. Our own lamps will burn the brighter for lighting others'. However, those who do not have the capacity of doing much good in conversation and can say little to edify others may yet hear that which will edify themselves. Those who cannot be teachers must be glad to be learners. Learners should visit those who are knowing and gracious with this intention: that they may improve themselves in knowledge and grace by conversation with them, and that by walking with wise men, they may be wise (Prov. 13:20). When Paul planned to visit his friends at Rome, he aimed both at their spiritual benefit and at his own. *"I long to see you, that I may impart unto you some spiritual gift...*[and] *that I may be comforted together with you"* (Rom. 1:11–12).

What we hear from the friends we visit that is instructive, and what we see in them that is exemplary and praiseworthy, we should take notice of and treasure up. We should use it when there is occasion. By conversing with those who are wise and good, we should strive to be made wiser and better. Some rules either of prudence, or piety, or both, we should gather up for our own use out of every visit. In this way, we may learn in everything to order our conduct rightly. As vain people make visits chiefly to see fashions, so serious people should make visits chiefly to learn wisdom. A wise man will thus hear and increase learning, and a man of understanding will by this means attain wise counsel (Prov. 1:5).

Even from what we hear and see that is foolish and blameworthy, we may learn that which will be profitable to us. Solomon received instruction even from the field of the slothful and the vine-yard of the man void of understanding. What we observe wrong in others, we must learn to avoid. Take warning from others' harms. Thus out of the eater may come forth meat, and out of the strong sweetness (Judg. 14:14).

Chapter 13

Correcting Our Conversation

*Let the words of my mouth, and the
meditation of my heart, be acceptable in thy
sight, O LORD, my strength, and my redeemer.*
—Psalm 19:14

I will conclude with a few words of exhortation. Let us all remember our faults this day and be humbled before God for the guilt we have contracted by our mismanaged visits of our friends.

In our common conversations as well as in our common business, it is hard to keep ourselves unspotted. Think of how much time we have lost in needless and unprofitable visits that might have been better bestowed and now cannot be recalled. What mean and low ends we have proposed to ourselves in making our visits, and how we have walked in them after the course of a vain and foolish world and not after the conduct of the law of the spirit of life in Christ Jesus. Are we not carnal, and do we not walk as men (1 Cor. 3:3)? Do we not fall far short of the spirit of Christianity, that high and holy calling with which we are called?

Think of how little good we have done in the visits we have made and received. How few have been the better because of us. It is well if many have not been the worse because of us and our corrupt communications. When our company has fallen into vain discourse, that foolish talking and jesting that the Word of God expressly condemns in Ephesians 5:4, have we not been as ready as any to promote it, keep it up, and show ourselves well pleased with it? Have we not provoked one another's lusts and passions instead of provoking one another to love and good works? Have we not given offense and put an occasion of stumbling in our brothers' ways by taking too great a liberty of speech with our friends, encouraging the hearts of the licentious in their looseness, and grieving the hearts of those who are serious themselves and expect us to be too? Let us for these things judge ourselves this day so that we may not be judged by the Lord.

Let us be so wise as to choose for our intimate friends those who will concur with us in a serious endeavor to get this matter mended. For the truth is, in this, as in a trade, we can make only one side of the bargain. We can only do a little toward rectifying what is amiss in conversation and toward improving it to some good purpose unless those we converse with will do their part. We should desire to associate ourselves with those who will edify us and be edified by us, whom we may either do good to, get good from, or both.

It is our wisdom to avoid the company that we find corrupts our minds, makes them vain, and indisposes them for serious exercises. What good we have in us is apt enough to dwindle and decay by itself. We do not need the help of others to quench it. Therefore, take Solomon's counsel: *"Go from the presence of a foolish man, when thou perceivest not in him the lips of knowledge"* (Prov. 14:7).

The communion of saints is intended to further our holiness and comfort. It is the pledge of our future bliss. We are taught by the pattern of the early church to continue steadfastly, not only in the apostles' doctrine but also in fellowship (Acts 2:42). Therefore, let us acquaint ourselves with some who appear to be serious Christians and converse with them. Let only such Christians be our bosom friends. Let us say to them, as the neighboring nations did to Israel: *"We will go with you: for we have heard that God is with you"* (Zech. 8:23). Let God's people be our people, and

David's resolution ours: *"I am a companion of all them that fear thee, and of them that keep thy precepts"* (Ps. 119:63).

Let us all resolve, by the grace of God, to keep a close watch on ourselves and on the condition of our own spirits in giving and receiving visits. If we cannot reform the world, I hope we may reform our own hearts and lives. Let every man examine his own work, and then he will rejoice in himself alone, though, perhaps, not in another (Gal. 6:4). So his praise will be of God, though perhaps not of men.

Christians, I am not persuading you to anything that is rude or morose. Nor am I speaking against the innocent diversions and entertainments of conversation, which are pleasant to yourselves and your friends and are a relief from the fatigue of business. But I am only reminding you that you must be very careful not to lose your religion in them. Remember that you are Christians, and everything you say and do must be fitting for saints. Remember that you are hastening into eternity: The days of your probation will soon be numbered and finished.

You must therefore spend your time on earth as those who are candidates and probationers for heaven so that you may not seem to come short. Converse with this world of the senses as those who know they must soon go to the world of spirits. Let this thought give a check to everything that is vain and empty. May it cause you to consider what sort of people you ought to be *"in all holy* [conduct] *and godliness"* (2 Pet. 3:11).

Lay before you therefore the example of the Lord Jesus. As He was, so let us be in this world. Let us walk as He walked. Let us make visits as He did, with every intention to do good, according to the sphere of our activities. His lips dripped honey and fed many. Let ours do so, too, as we are able.

Wherever Jesus was, He was about His Father's business. Let us, though unworthy of such an honor, still endeavor to be likewise employed. When He visited His friends, He sympathized with them in their griefs, comforted them under their afflictions, reproved them for what was amiss, and entertained them with edifying and instructive discourses. He often used common occurrences in His discourses. His speech was admirable yet imitable. These things are written for our learning. *"Go, and do thou likewise"* (Luke 10:37).

So that we may be thoroughly furnished, like the good householder who brings out of his treasury new and old, let us daily pray to God for that wisdom of the prudent, which is to understand his way in everything. There is no one grace that we are more particularly directed and encouraged to pray for than this. If any man lacks wisdom (and which of us does not?), let him ask it of God, who gives liberally and does not reproach us for our former follies, our present necessities, or the frequency of our requests. (See James 1:5.)

Solomon, who in his youth made wisdom his choice and request, had that granted to him, along with an abundance of other good things. In making this petition, let us therefore be not only constant and earnest but also very particular. Lord, give me wisdom that will direct me in cases that are difficult and doubtful. Lord, enable me to behave wisely in a perfect way toward my family and toward my friends and neighbors whom I visit. Help me also to walk in wisdom toward those who are outsiders. Help me, Lord, so that my profession of religion and relation to Christ may never suffer damage or reproach through any imprudence or indiscretion of mine, in any visit given or received.

Lest this wisdom should degenerate into that which is worldly and err by an excess of caution, let us pray to God for a spirit of holy boldness and courage also. With such boldness, we will be enabled to appear and act for God and godliness in all companies and on all occasions. We will have that pious zeal that suits the good soldiers of Jesus Christ. May all those we converse with see that we serve a Master whom we are neither ashamed nor afraid to acknowledge. May they see that we have ventured all our credit with men, upon the security of that promise of God: *"Them that honour me I will honour"* (1 Sam. 2:30).

About the Author

I n a Welsh farmhouse on October 18, 1662, a frail child entered the world. His name was Matthew Henry. He was so sick that he was not expected to live even a week. But God preserved the life of this little baby who would grow up to do great things for Him. Matthew continued to be physically weak as a child, but mentally he grew stronger and stronger. At three years of age, he is said to have read aloud a chapter from the Bible.

Indeed, his love for the Bible must have begun at an early age. His parents' home was known for its godliness; it was called "a house of God and a gate of heaven." His father, Philip Henry, was well known as a clergyman. He was a Dissenter (because he dissented from the Act of Uniformity that was laid down by the church) and therefore received no salary, but he served his congregation unselfishly.

Philip Henry was gifted as a scholar and teacher, and he taught Matthew until he was eighteen years old. Then Matthew attended the academy in Islington, London. Although it was often persecuted as a "dissenting academy," it was an outstanding educational institution.

Matthew Henry attended the academy for two years and later studied law. With his incredible memory and admirable eloquence, he easily could have been a successful lawyer. However, he chose to follow in his father's footsteps and became a pastor. From 1687 to 1712, he pastored a church in Chester, and then he had a church in London until his death.

Matthew Henry had a very happy and precious home life, in spite of several tragedies. His first wife died of smallpox, and three of his nine children by his second wife died in infancy. Much of the joy of his home life, no doubt, can be attributed to his faithfulness to morning and evening devotions.

Much of what he wrote in his well-known *Commentary on the Bible* was on outgrowth of these devotions with family and neighbors. Perhaps that is much of the reason for the practical nature of this work, for it teaches lessons on how to live. It has been teaching Christians for over two and a half centuries, and some of the best-known preachers have relied on it. George

Whitefield read this six-volume commentary four times.

Matthew Henry was only fifty-two years old when he died from apoplexy in 1714. But he left behind a legacy that has not been forgotten.

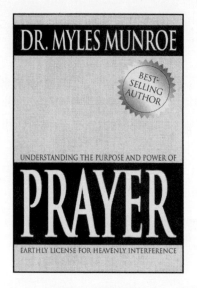

Understanding the Purpose and Power of Prayer
Dr. Myles Munroe

All that God is—and all that God has—may be received
through prayer. Everything you need to fulfill your
purpose on earth is available to you through prayer.
The biblically based, time-tested principles presented
here by Dr. Myles Munroe will ignite and transform
the way you pray. Be prepared to enter into a new
dimension of faith, a deeper revelation of God's
love, and a renewed understanding that
you can pray—and receive results.

ISBN: 0-88368-442-X • Trade • 240 pages

ш

WHITAKER
HOUSE

proclaiming the power of the Gospel through the written word
visit our website at www.whitakerhouse.com

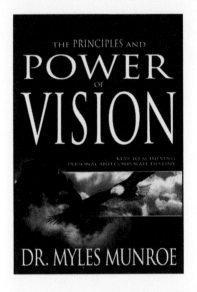

The Principles and Power of Vision
Dr. Myles Munroe

Whether you are a businessperson, a homemaker, a student, or a head of state, best-selling author Dr. Myles Munroe explains how you can make your dreams and hopes a living reality. Your success is not dependent on the state of the economy or what the job market is like. You do not need to be hindered by the limited perceptions of others or by a lack of resources. Discover time-tested principles that will enable you to fulfill your vision no matter who you are or where you come from.

ISBN: 0-88368-951-0 • Hardcover • 240 pages

ɯɯ
WHITAKER
HOUSE

proclaiming the power of the Gospel through the written word
visit our website at www.whitakerhouse.com

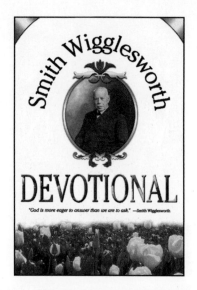

Smith Wigglesworth Devotional
Smith Wigglesworth

You are invited to journey with Smith Wigglesworth on a year-long trip that will quench your spiritual thirst while it radically transforms your faith. As you daily explore these challenging insights from the Apostle of Faith, you will connect with God's glorious power, cast out doubt, and see impossibilities turn into realities. Your prayer life will never be the same again when you personally experience the joy of seeing awesome, powerful results as you extend God's healing grace to others.

ISBN: 0-88368-574-4 • Trade • 560 pages

W
WHITAKER
HOUSE

proclaiming the power of the Gospel through the written word
visit our website at www.whitakerhouse.com

The Practice of God's Presence
Andrew Murray

Is something missing in your Christian life? Do you long to become the person God wants you to be, to feel His presence and experience His power? Andrew Murray's scriptural insights make it easy for you to know God. Learn how to have a dynamic, joy-filled relationship with the Lord. Live every day, every hour, in intimate fellowship with Him. In this collection of six of Murray's best-sellers, you will discover that not only can you have an effective prayer life, but you can also experience the fullness of the Holy Spirit, a blameless heart, and victory over sin.

ISBN: 0-88368-590-6 • Trade • 576 pages

ɯ
WHITAKER
HOUSE

proclaiming the power of the Gospel through the written word
visit our website at www.whitakerhouse.com

You hunger to live in the presence of God. You yearn to know the Father's heart in an intimate way. You desire revelation and passionate encounters with the Almighty. You want to spend time away from the world, getting to know the Father in a deeper way. If you long to experience a greater intimacy with the Father, *The Secret Place* will draw you in and change your life!

The Secret Place: Passionately Pursuing His Presence
Dr. Dale A. Fife
ISBN: 0-88368-715-1 • Trade • 240 pages

The Hidden Kingdom: Journey into the Heart of God
Dr. Dale A. Fife
ISBN: 0-88368-947-2 • Trade • 256 pages

There are divine moments in life when you turn a corner and are astounded by unexpected, breathtaking vistas that you never imagined. Suddenly your world is changed forever. You have entered a supernatural realm, an eternal dimension, where Jesus is Lord and creation itself shouts His glory. The brilliantly illuminating revelation in *The Hidden Kingdom* will catapult you into such an experience. If you want an empowered life, this book will lead you on a journey into the heart of God.

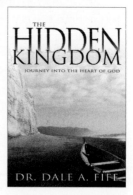

WHITAKER HOUSE

proclaiming the power of the Gospel through the written word
visit our website at www.whitakerhouse.com